PRAISE FOR
EPIC PERFORMANCE

"Anytime you want to be at your best, you need a vision of where you will go, a strategy for how you will get there, and a clear mind to keep you focused. *EPIC Performance* gives you that road map and guides you so you don't get distracted by the shiny objects."

BRET HEDICAN
NHL STANLEY CUP WINNER; TWO-TIME OLYMPIAN; SAN JOSE SHARKS BROADCASTER

"If you are a dreamer who is committed to taking action, *EPIC Performance* is a must-read! Bryan lays out a plan of purpose, inspiration, grit, and determination that will transform your mindset from 'I wish I would have...' to 'I'm glad I did....'"

PAUL EPSTEIN
FORMER NFL AND NBA EXECUTIVE, BESTSELLING AUTHOR OF *THE POWER OF PLAYING OFFENSE*

"*EPIC Performance* is a great read with practical advice wrapped around an inspirational story. If you are looking to take that next step in your organization or your life, this book will help you reach higher and achieve extraordinary results."

LAILA TARRAF
FORMER CHIEF PEOPLE OFFICER, ALLBIRDS AND, PEET'S COFFEE & TEA, AND BESTSELLING
AUTHOR OF *STRONG LIKE WATER*

"Reaching an epic goal or peak performance is easier said than done. *EPIC Performance* gives readers all the tools, action plans, and encouragement to do nothing less. When you finish reading this book, you will be excited to take the first steps that can and will eventually lead to reaching your own epic goal."

JULIETTE GOODRICH

CBS NEWS ANCHOR/REPORTER

"Starting my first company was an exciting but scary prospect. *EPIC Performance* provides an excellent framework for moving toward and through these crucial and frightening moments by building on your innate drive, determination, and vision. I wish I had these insights back then."

JOHN NEWTON

FOUNDER, DOCUMENTUM AND ALFRESCO

"When I find myself having to work through critical decisions, I focus on the best-case scenario—not the worst-case. That's why I love the framework in *EPIC Performance*. This book will help readers reframe their approach to taking on new opportunities or challenges both personally and professionally. Plus, any book that quotes *Dumb and Dumber* is a book that I want to read. I use the 'so you're telling me there's a chance' quote all the time because it centers on the possible, just as Bryan outlines."

JULIE CULLIVAN

FORMER CHIEF TECHNOLOGY OFFICER AND CHIEF PEOPLE OFFICER, FORESCOUT TECHNOLOGIES

"*EPIC Performance* provides a road map for results and is a must-read for any executive looking to flex their superpowers in their personal and professional life."

AILA MALIK
FOUNDER, VENTURE LEADERSHIP CONSULTING, AND AUTHOR

"It's easy to dream big, but most people don't know how to start putting it into action. *EPIC Performance* is an amazing and inspirational set of stories and experiences turned into an actionable guide for achieving your dreams."

WHITNEY BOUCK
MANAGING DIRECTOR, INSIGHT PARTNERS, AND FORMER COO, HELLOSIGN

"*EPIC Performance* offers a fresh view of what it takes to achieve the most ambitious of goals. As a longtime endurance athlete who has recently realized a lifelong dream of starting a business, I found it to be a realistic and motivating look at how to make the impossible possible."

JEFF ROSENTHAL
FOUNDER AND CO-CEO, PROJECTNEXT LEADERSHIP, AND
FORMER CEO, UC BERKELEY CENTER FOR EXECUTIVE EDUCATION

"*EPIC Performance* is brilliantly written, carefully researched, and all-encompassing. Bryan Gillette takes the reader through the five pillars of success—allowing us to not only believe we can reach higher but offering strategies to achieve those goals. A must-read for those wishing to succeed in fulfilling their wildest dreams."

DIANN BOYLE
UNITED STATES AIR FORCE PILOT AND CAPTAIN, SOUTHWEST AIRLINES (RETIRED)

"Why keep setting limits for yourself? *EPIC Performance* provides a proven process for envisioning then reaching your own epic goals. Take a chance, light that fire inside you, and go do something epic."

JIM MOONEY
FORMER GENERAL MANAGER, MARKETING, TOYOTA NORTH AMERICA, AND EXECUTIVE COACH

"This is a damn good book. After reading this, I immediately used a few of the concepts and found the stories to be inspirational."

JERRY PENTIN
PRODUCER/DIRECTOR, SPRING STREET STUDIOS

"*EPIC Performance* captures the top-line reasons for success and provides you with insights that Bryan Gillette has gleaned from many years of coaching and learning from winners."

BARRY BROOME
PRESIDENT & CEO, GREATER SACRAMENTO ECONOMIC COUNCIL,
AND FORMER CEO, GREATER PHOENIX ECONOMIC COUNCIL

"*EPIC Performance* is one of the most practical and motivating books ever written on maximizing human potential. It analyzes the skills and behaviors of one hundred successful executives and high-performing individuals and offers a road map for others to replicate their successes."

MIKE FRECCERO
PRINCIPAL, TORCHIANA, MASTROV & SAPIRO, AND FORMER EXECUTIVE COACH

"The five pillars of *EPIC Performance* provided a framework to help me swim twenty-one miles in open water across Lake Tahoe—one of my greatest accomplishments!"

JORGE ANGEL
SALES EXECUTIVE, AMAZON AND ORACLE AND SUN MICROSYSTEMS, AND ELITE ULTRADISTANCE SWIMMER

"This well-researched guide will help you create an epic life. No one wants mediocrity—I don't. *EPIC Performance* is filled with great anecdotes, solid research, and—most importantly—practical advice and exercises that will help you achieve success in whatever aspect of life is important to you. I've read many books in the field of performance, and this is one of the best!"

TIM WEYLAND

SENIOR VICE PRESIDENT, HUMAN RESOURCES, TOPCON POSITIONING SYSTEMS; FIFA REFEREE; IRONMAN

"As you'll discover in *EPIC Performance*, Bryan has accomplished many amazing things by bringing out the best in himself—and he truly understands how to bring out the very best in others. He's a great leader and coach."

JOE GABBERT, PHD

FORMER EXECUTIVE VICE PRESIDENT, HUMAN RESOURCES, MCAFEE AND DOCUMENTUM

"As some people reach the midpoint of their careers, they have a tendency to believe that learning is limited to 'trial and error.' If that describes you, grab *EPIC Performance* and flip it open. Read a few pages to gain both learning and inspiration, and you'll likely end up reading it cover to cover, like I did."

CHRIS HENRY

FORMER GLOBAL SALES CORPORATE VICE PRESIDENT, XILINX

"*EPIC Performance* is a practical playbook and a perfect gift to anyone thinking about and wanting to do big things."

RON REL

WORLD-CLASS OFF-ROAD ULTRAENDURANCE ATHLETE AND CYBER SECURITY EVANGELIST

"In *EPIC Performance*, Bryan Gillette provides a motivational, step-by-step guide to dreaming bigger and successfully achieving professional and personal goals even beyond our own expectations. Be ready to be inspired, to laugh, and to find yourself stepping up the corporate ladder to a more fulfilling life in which dreams really do come true."

JIM OTT, EDD
COLLEGE ENGLISH PROFESSOR AND FORMER CEO, UNCLE CREDIT UNION

"Most leaders' life journeys are filled with ascents and descents. The framework revealed in *EPIC Performance* allows us to recognize the stage we are in, consider course corrections, and put ourselves in the right frame of mind to continue the journey. I'm grateful for the simplicity—and power—of this book."

RANDY HAYKIN
SERIAL ENTREPRENEUR; VENTURE CAPITALIST; FOUNDER, THE GRATITUDE NETWORK

"*EPIC Performance* serves as an effective toolbox for someone to take their vision and turn it into reality. Bryan Gillette has spoken to my executive team several times, and—after learning the five pillars of EPIC Performance—my staff was able to achieve some extraordinary goals."

JAMES LIM
SENIOR VICE PRESIDENT, SUNLAND RV RESORTS,
AND FORMER GENERAL MANAGER, OMNI HOTELS & RESORTS

"This book is an essential read for anyone striving to achieve their lifelong goals. *EPIC Performance* shows how growth is outside the comfort zone, and it gives you the tools to get there."

BILL WHEELER
PRESIDENT AND CEO, BLACK TIE TRANSPORTATION

www.amplifypublishing.com

EPIC Performance: Lessons from 100 Executives & Endurance Athletes on Reaching Your Peak

For more information, please contact Amplify Publishing
620 Herndon Parkway #320
Herndon, VA 20170
info@amplifypublishing.com

Credit for author photo: Jerry Pentin

Library of Congress Control Number: 2021920919

CPSIA Code: PRV0222A
ISBN-13: 978-1-63755-217-9

Printed in the United States

*I dedicate this book to
my parents, my wife,
and my two boys.*

EPIC
PERFORMANCE

Lessons from 100 Executives & Endurance Athletes on Reaching Your Peak

BRYAN GILLETTE

PRESIDENT OF SUMMITING GROUP

Contents

Foreword

As the former CEO of McAfee, FireEye, and Documentum and a former All-American college wrestler, pushing the limits has always been a cornerstone of who I am. It also defines the type of executives I hire and the people I surround myself with every day.

That determination and drive was instilled in me early on from my parents. We didn't have a lot of money, but they encouraged me and my brother to be the first ones in our family to go to college, push ourselves, and live a life better than they did. This set a tone for my life to this day.

This is why *EPIC Performance* resonates so much with me. I love how Bryan outlines a practical way to push ourselves in the right direction and go further than we might have imagined. I love how he shows readers how to envision the future then go after it. And I also love how he combines the arenas of sport and business, because people who achieve extraordinary accomplishments in one field often do the same in another. My early successes competing against the best wrestlers in the nation clearly prepared me to succeed in the corporate world.

As an executive and ultradistance athlete, Bryan knows what it is like to dream big and then persevere to some extreme finish lines. We first met more than twenty years ago. I was leading engineering for Documentum—a $200 million software company at the time—and he was overseeing leadership development.

Within two years of my arrival at Documentum, I took over as CEO and relied on him to make sure I had the right tools in place for me to succeed. I was learning the ropes and fortunate to have many extraordinary people around me—Bryan being one. He is a strong leader and an excellent coach.

While I have seen what he can do at work, I have been equally impressed with his performance in ultradistance events. He has undertaken some crazy endeavors—running eight marathons back-to-back being one of the biggest.

But his research for this book went far beyond his own experiences. I've been fortunate to work with a handful of the impressive executives who were interviewed for this book and have seen how many of those executives use the elements of Bryan's unique and easily understandable EPIC Performance framework in practice. I also apply many of these techniques every day, and I can tell you that they work and helped get me to where I am today.

Most people want to look back over their time on Earth and feel like they have made a difference and reached higher. This book shows you how.

DAVE DEWALT
Former CEO of Documentum, McAfee, and FireEye
Founder/CEO of NightDragon

Preface

I F I SAID YOU COULD RUN EIGHT MARATHONS back-to-back on remote dirt trails with only ninety minutes of sleep in seventy-six hours through the Sierra Nevada mountain range, you might say I was crazy and that you could never do it. While you may be right about the first part, don't underestimate what you can do. Trust me. It is doable.

I know because I did it.

I am guessing you have dreamed of something big and thought, "I wish I could do that…"—but something stopped you. You wanted to start a business, retire early, pursue a different career, grow revenue exponentially, write a book, run a marathon, or travel the world. Whether it was lack of money, time, skill, fear, or whatever, something held you back. It is that idea you had ten years ago, which then popped into your head five years ago and then again in the last year. Now you're asking, "Should I still do it?"

The clock is moving fast, and at some point, it may be too late; you may regret never having chased your dream. If that is you, read on because now may be the time.

Unfortunately—or perhaps fortunately—we do not know when the end arrives. The average life span is 76 years for men and 81 years for women. My wife's two grandmothers lived to 101, but her dad died at 32 from a rare form of cancer. His sister died by a drunk driver in college. So saying, "I am going to [INSERT YOUR DREAM HERE] later or when I retire" could be a mistake. Later is not guaranteed and may be too late. We have all heard the stories where someone retires with plans to travel the world and then dies within the year. With the average retirement age being 62, that does not leave you a lot of time to reach some of those bucket list items.

So let's bring those big dreams to the front of your head now and set a plan to carry them out soon. In this book, I will share how I and over a hundred others whom I have interviewed have done this. And you can too.

ASKING THE EXPERTS HOW THEY ACHIEVED EXTRAORDINARY RESULTS

For most of my career, I have coached individual contributors, leaders, and teams on how to maximize performance. I have seen the difference between people who quickly move up the ladder and those who stagnate at their desk. I have found that those who do well in their careers often challenge themselves in their personal lives as well. And through all this time, I have wanted to understand two basic questions:

1. What are the skills or behaviors needed to achieve extraordinary results?
2. Can these skills transfer among business, sport, career, and life?

Personally, I have completed my share of big goals—from cycling four thousand miles across the United States to running two hundred miles around Lake Tahoe to traveling twice around the world for an extended period of time to starting up my own business.

While I am proud of my accomplishments, I wanted to understand what other successful leaders, entrepreneurs, athletes, and businesspeople do as well. I set out to find that answer and learn the different steps that lead to a winning outcome. This led me down the path to having amazing conversations with over a hundred successful people who have accomplished some extraordinary goals. And along the way, I was humbled by what I heard.

These people have been CEOs of billion-dollar companies, Ironman coaches, venture capitalists, ultradistance runners, company founders, executive coaches, authors, and educators. They have bootstrapped a company from a few dollars and passion for their idea, then sold it for billions. They have cycled from Cairo, Egypt, in the north of Africa 7,500 miles south to Cape Town, South Africa. They have started a company, then pivoted when their idea was too early to market, then pivoted again. Some have been titans in their industry and worked with some of the smartest people in the room. Some have been the smartest person in the room with PhDs and other advanced degrees, and some never started college.

And while diverse in their accomplishments, careers, genders, educations, and ethnicities, there are common threads among them all. They all have had big dreams and successfully turned those dreams into reality. They have all failed at times, learned from their mistakes, and moved forward. They experience insecurities, nervousness, or anxiety at times— just like me and maybe you. And surprisingly, there was a humility with most. Many did not think their accomplishments were big enough and asked, "Why do you want to talk with me?" And then after I asked, "How many people have [FILL IN THEIR ACCOMPLISHMENT]?" they thought, nodded in agreement, and openly responded to my questions. In some cases, I will use actual names and companies, while for others I will leave out their name to honor their request for confidentiality.

I also researched and talked with psychologists who study the mind. I took my more than a hundred interviews and compared those perspectives with the researchers' academic work to develop my own framework for success. People who reach the top of a mountain peak or the highest point in their profession, or cross a finish line and raise their hands in victory, do it through the five pillars of EPIC Performance. You can too.

From this book, you will learn about these pillars and practical tips to replicate in your own life, so you move your dreams from "**I can't**" to "**I DID!**"

THE FIVE PILLARS OF EPIC PERFORMANCE

ENVISION the dreams you have for your career, your company, and your life. This involves knowing your values and purpose, developing a strategy to dream bigger, and learning to stretch yourself into more uncomfortable zones.

PLAN to make those dreams become reality by setting a path to achieve them. The first thing is to start. Start doing something that moves you closer to your goal. Often this first step is developing a plan. Then begin assessing your obstacles and risks.

ITERATE your plan to work out the kinks and scale your accomplishments. With a solid plan already developed, now it is time to focus on the tasks. This is a chance to assess your progress by practicing and looking at key data points, then dealing with the problems as they arise.

COLLABORATE with others to learn from the successes and failures of those before you. Most things in life have already been done, so learn from the experts. Surround yourself with key advisors who can help you focus on the right areas. And if this is more than a solo effort (few are), make sure you have a solid team that is prepared to support you.

Perform by putting your plan, learnings, and experiences into action and running to the finish line. When it gets difficult and you do not know what to do, refocus on the plan and your overall goal. Perseverance will get you through the challenging times. And once you have successfully reached the "finish line," reward yourself and start thinking about the two most glorious words in the English language for successful people: What's next?

These pillars will provide you with a framework to start thinking beyond what you are accustomed to, but they will not eliminate the hard work. Be skeptical of anybody or any book that claims to tell you how to get rich quick, lose one hundred pounds fast, or achieve success overnight—their advice is either too risky, unsafe, or highly unlikely to be effective. Generally, the only person who will get rich from these schemes is the person who is trying to sell you on their concept. Never underestimate the power of hard work, long hours, and grit. They often generate tremendous results. More on that later.

Dreaming "big" is a relative term, so my goal is to help you to dream *bigger*. Bigger than what you may have thought yesterday. Bigger than what others may think you can do. And most important, bigger than what you believe you can do. Keep in mind that there will always be someone who has done, or can do, more. Don't compare your achievements to what others have achieved and see them as a threat. View their victories as an opportunity to see what the human mind and body are capable of—and let them inspire you even more.

WHY SHOULD YOU READ THIS BOOK?

I have read a lot of books about survival and one's ability to endure tremendous pain and suffering, including *Endurance: Shackleton's Incredible Voyage* (Alfred Lansing), *Into Thin Air* (Jon Krakauer), *Touching the Void* (Joe Simpson), *Alive* (Piers Paul Read), *The Pursuit of Happyness* (Chris Gardner), *Deep Down Dark* (Héctor Tobar), *We Die Alone* (David Howarth), and *Unbroken: A World War II Story of Survival, Resilience, and Redemption* (Laura Hillenbrand).

Most of these incredible stories show determination, grit, and sheer willpower. In most cases, failure meant death. In some cases, people lost limbs, were forever psychologically scarred, or saw friends die.

In reality, what many of us go through is not about life or death but about living or subsisting. It is about intentionally putting yourself in new or uncomfortable situations. It is about being purposeful about the life you live versus the life you want to live. Don't let randomness determine your path. When failure occurs, it likely means a bruised ego, sore muscles, a smaller bank account, a delayed promotion, or lost time. For most, it rarely means death.

Of course, there are limits to the risks most of us are willing to take. I watched an interview on *60 Minutes*[1] years ago about risk-takers who jump off cliffs with wingsuits and fly through rock formations to then skydive to the ground. The program also featured people who free climb up El Capitan in Yosemite, which is without a rope or any safety devices. The interviewer asked if they felt like they were risking their lives and would die. They responded that they didn't feel alive unless they were doing these extreme activities. While mortality is guaranteed for everyone, these people tend to see it earlier than most. We must all understand how much risk we are willing to take. But keep in mind, risk is something that can be broken down and managed— which we will explore.

I have traveled extensively twice around the world in my life. First with my soon-to-be wife for seven months through New Zealand, Australia, Southeast Asia, and China, where I proposed on the Great Wall. And second, for a year with my wife and two boys through South America, Africa, and the Middle East. Before we left and upon our return, we heard from so many people saying, "I wish I could do that." Some of those people did not mean it. Many truly wished they could but did not know how. This book is for the latter.

My heart goes out to those who say "I wish I could…" because for so many people, they likely could. This book is for you. It is also for my two boys so they realize they can push themselves beyond what they ever have imagined. When I was twenty years old, I got on my bike and cycled four thousand miles by myself from Newport, Oregon, to Newport, Rhode Island. It was before cell phones, so every few days I would find a pay phone and call home to let my parents know where I was, and more importantly that I was alive. I am sure they worried every day. I am sure there was a massive part of them that wished I stayed home where it was "safe." But they encouraged me despite the emotional distress they were going through.

It seems that as a society we are wrapping our kids in bubble wrap so they never get hurt. Those kids then grow up and don't take off the bubble wrap. As my kids get older and want to go out and explore the world, I will feel the same. I will be nervous but must remember how my parents treated me. I must let my boys explore, make mistakes, and push the limits. And while it will make me uneasy, I must remember that for fifty days during the summer of 1988, my parents did not sleep much while I was on an adventure of a lifetime. Life is about doing things now so in thirty years you will say, "I'm sure glad I did…"—and more importantly that you do not say, "I wish I would have…."

How to Use This Book

FOR THOSE OF YOU WHO LIKE TO fully read an instruction manual before starting to assemble your recent purchase, you may choose to read the book from start to finish. And for those of you who only rely on the manual when you get stuck, consider taking the EPIC Performance Assessment highlighted at the end of this section to focus your time on specific chapters. Then, scan the Activities section at the end of each chapter to help define your next steps. Either way, the book should be a resource to help you dream a little bit bigger than you did yesterday.

It includes tips and ideas to increase your ability to succeed and go further than before. What I have learned from my thirty years working in different companies and for different leaders and watching accomplished people excel is that there are many paths to success. I have read business books that suggest one strategy. I have also watched people do the complete opposite and still be phenomenally successful. However, some strategies have consistently proven effective, and—as you'll see—those were borne out in the advice of the interview subjects you will meet throughout these pages. Use their expertise and experience, then prioritize what will work best for you. They provide inspiration and edification for you to get where you want to go and, I'm hopeful, a bit further than you thought you could. Choose a strategy and try it. And if it works, use it again. If it does not work, reflect and try to figure out why. If you do not have a conclusive answer, move on.

Each main topic, or pillar, of this book (Envision / Plan / Iterate / Collaborate / Perform) consists of three sections:

1. Overview of the pillar.
2. Descriptive behaviors and strategies to develop in this area.
3. Questions and exercises to get you thinking and propel you forward.

By buying this book, you are entitled to the EPIC Performance Assessment, which evaluates you on the five pillars and fifteen corresponding behaviors. From the results, you will better see your strengths and development areas. To access the assessment, go to:

ASSESSMENT: EPICPERFORMANCES.COM
COMPANY CODE: EPICBOOK

If this book helped you, or if you would like further guidance on your EPIC journey, go to www.epicperformances.com or contact Bryan's organization at info@epicperformances.com.

Prologue

BEARS, BEARS, EVERYWHERE!

I WAS 164 MILES INTO A 205-MILE RUN on the remote and rugged dirt trails circling Lake Tahoe in the Sierra Nevada mountain range. This beautiful lake, straddling California and Nevada, is the largest alpine lake in North America and only behind the Great Lakes in terms of volume. I had endured two sleepless nights and was entering my third evening in the pitch black as we moved through a dark and lonely section when the runner in front of me—one of two people within miles—screamed, "Stop!" It was clear by the fear in his voice that something was terribly wrong. I abruptly halted. And then he said, "There is an animal out there. Move back very slowly."

As I inched my way over to the other person in our triad, Bruce—a friend who was pacing me on this section—stepped closer and put his hand on my shoulder to ease my fears. Pacers join for part of the race and help navigate the trail, remind you to eat and drink, and make sure you are mentally and physically able to continue. One could question (and many have) whether someone is mentally stable when they voluntarily sign up to run 205 miles. Heck, you may be questioning my sanity. However, a pacer knows you are nuts but believes in your dream anyway. They too may have done something similar and have confidence in your success.

Whatever the reason, Bruce had joined me about ten miles earlier and had fresh legs and an alert mind. The three of us stood close to each other with the intent to look bigger—we hoped to look like more of a threat than dinner to whatever massive beast stood in our way. We were in bear territory and couldn't see our angry rival. I had been seeing "bears" throughout the evening, or at least what I thought were bears. Given my lack of sleep and sheer exhaustion, every time I came across a tree stump or a large rock, I momentarily panicked until I realized what was in front of me.

But this time the threat was real as we saw its eyes when we aimed our headlamps down the hill about one hundred feet. The reflection of two white, beady eyeballs staring back confirmed it was not a mirage like the other "bears" I had been seeing for hours. The other runner said, "Cat," which caused me to first think jaguar, lion, tiger, or cheetah. My heart rate elevated.

A rational and coherent person would know that these felines are not present in this area. I had been awake for almost sixty hours and had run the equivalent of six back-to-back marathons at this point; I could hardly be classified as either rational or coherent. What then went through my head was that Bruce and I had come across the other runner about half an hour earlier, and he was in a lot of pain and moving very slowly—more pain than I was experiencing and more slowly than I was moving. My mind quickly went to that joke about two hikers seeing a bear, and one stops to lace up his running shoes. The other hiker says, "What are you doing? You can't outrun a bear!" The other responds, "I don't have to outrun the bear. I just need to outrun you." With Bruce in the best condition after running only (!) ten miles, he could outrun me. I was in better shape than the other runner and could outrun him if the animal started to attack. For a moment, I was relieved. I realize this may have been a bit macabre, but keep in mind my mental state was not at its highest. My heartbeat dropped a little but was still thumping at an unsustainable rate.

For what seemed like an hour—but was likely thirty seconds, or maybe five—we assessed the situation.

Bruce, being of sound mind and body, said, "Don't worry, it's just a deer."

"Are you sure?" I asked.

He looked a little harder and confirmed that it was just a deer. My heart rate dropped to a reasonable level as the three of us cautiously and safely continued down the trail past our immediate threat: Bambi.

Two more marathons to the finish line.

Running 205 miles is no easy task. It is made even more difficult when the elevation ranges from 5,500 feet to almost 10,000 feet above sea level and consists of over 40,000 feet of vertical elevation gain. To put this in perspective, Mount Everest is 29,032 feet above sea level. Or imagine running to the top of the Empire State Building and then back to the bottom thirty-two times. This run has a lot of uphill.

While physically challenging, the mental component is far more difficult. It pushes a person to limits few people see, which for many of us is the allure. Sir Edmund Hillary summed it up best when asked why he would climb Everest: "Because it is there," he replied. While there is more to reaching your peak, it is a start.

THE GENESIS OF EPIC PERFORMANCE

For most of my life, I have chosen goals—whether for work, career, personal growth, sport, or health—that have tested and challenged me. I have taken on projects at work that had failed before or started up new departments with nothing but an idea. I like challenges. They push me. They test me. They make me stronger and smarter than before. They also make me realize there is so much more to learn.

Several years before running around Lake Tahoe, I was looking for a challenge—something that would push me physically and get me out on my bike but also something that would test me mentally and emotionally. I had done many one- and two-hundred-mile bike rides with few problems, so I needed something bigger. What about riding three hundred miles, through the night, to be my first twenty-four-hour endurance event? I wondered how far my body could go, or when my mind would say, "I'm done." This, I thought, would be that test. I planned to ride in an organized two-hundred-mile ride, and then at the finish line, I would continue—into the night and by myself—another one hundred miles.

It was a long, hot day, and I was frustrated and shaken when another cyclist careened into me, causing my front wheel to resemble the shape of an S. After getting a new wheel and continuing down the road another 30 miles, my problems were put into perspective when I came across several fire trucks and police cars and an ambulance. A fellow rider, lying on the side of the road and covered by a blanket, was dead. I found out later that he died of a heart attack. I was stunned. That image sat with me for the next 170 miles as I wondered if it was worth continuing the ride. Am I pushing myself too much? Am I risking the well-being of my wife and kids? Is this worth it?

But, well into the early hours and after 275 miles of hard riding, the finish line was easily within sight when those questions were answered.

I never hit "The Wall." It was at that point that I realized that my mind and body are far more powerful than I gave them credit for. I also realized that we often say, "I can't do [FILL IN BLANK]" and give up too easily. But, just maybe, we can. As I approached the end of that three-hundred-mile, twenty-four-hour bike ride, my mind was racing for what was next: a marathon.

I was never a runner. As a kid, when others were sprinting around the field, I was slowly taking up the rear. My parents used to joke that most kids were timed with a stopwatch, but they used a calendar with me. We all have our strengths; running just wasn't mine. So why would I even think of a marathon, you ask? Because the marathon is often considered the ultimate running goal and one many aspire to finish. While I knew I was in decent shape from cycling, I had never come close to running 26.2 miles. So I did what I always do with a goal: I set a plan and started small.

As I was working from home one day, I went out at lunch and bought a pair of shoes at our local running store and went for a four-mile run. It felt great—that is, until I completed my afternoon conference call and had to walk upstairs. Ouch. My legs were killing me. As a strong cyclist who relies on strong leg muscles, I felt running four miles would be no problem because I am using the same legs. I quickly learned how different cycling and running are. While running a marathon is not, and was not, easy, I had had the confidence that I could do it after completing many other similarly difficult events.

With all goals, it means starting off small and building. Running a marathon was no different. That week's long run was four miles. The next week's would be five. Then six and so on. A few months later it was 26.2 when I crossed the finish line near the Golden Gate Bridge in San Francisco. Within a few months, while sitting around a table with friends, we talked about what was next—a 50-mile trail run. Shortly after that, it was another 50-mile run, with several more to follow before jumping to 100 miles. And then 205 miles. That is when this book started to form.

MUSCLES STRETCHED AND MUSCLES STRAINED

If there ever was a time to show that we can go further, think of the spring of 2020. Much of the United States, and the world, shut down to flatten the coronavirus curve. An international Work from Home (WFH) policy was mandated overnight, and so many countries and companies rose to the challenge, mainly because they did not have a choice. A few weeks before the mandatory WFH policy was implemented, if a CEO told her leadership team everyone needs to be able to work from home 100 percent of the time, her staff would have laughed and said, "That's impossible. We can't do that."

The more optimistic leaders would have said, "That's probably going to take a year to implement." But so many did this in a matter of days. Teachers began educating students from home. Theatre directors resumed rehearsal from home. City building inspectors reviewed properties and started signing permits from home. Winemakers conducted flight tastings from home. So many people did what they said could never be done. The "impossible" was proven possible.

Making massive shifts, like moving mountains, requires a lot of muscle. When forced, that muscle is strained. And though it may be injured in the process, it will likely come back, especially if that muscle was well trained, flexible, and given time to get stronger and more resilient. Some of the injuries were permanent, as businesses crumbled or individuals cracked. But many came out stronger.

Any muscle can be strengthened over time. Instead of waiting until you are forced to stretch that muscle and risk long-term injury, build it up over the course of months, years, or decades.

But it does take time.

YOU CAN BE WHATEVER YOU WANT TO BE—NOT!

Don't kid yourself: you can't be whatever you want to be. I love the saying "You can be whatever you want to be" because it makes me feel like I can do anything. Alas, I cannot.

I have ruled out wearing the Yellow Jersey—indicating the leader—in the Tour de France. I remember being glued to the TV as Greg LeMond raced into Paris and became the first American to win that European-dominated sport. Even at twenty-one years old, I dreamed of holding that coveted trophy while standing on the Champs-Élysées with the Arc de Triomphe in the background. Given that Lance Armstrong and Floyd Landis have been stripped of their wins (see kids, you should not do drugs), maybe I could be the second American to win. Um, probably not. I'm in my fifties. Statistically, I will not be racing in the Tour de France—ever. The physiological peak of an elite cyclist is the mid- to late twenties. Since the average age of a Tour winner is twenty-eight (1903–2012)[2] and the oldest was thirty-six years old (1922), I am playing the odds and focusing my goals elsewhere.

When I asked several highly successful people if they believed the adage "You can do anything," they responded unanimously with some form of no. They didn't hesitate. A successful middle-aged venture capitalist said, "That's bullshit. I'd love to be a model in New York City, but that ain't happening." Julie Cullivan—former chief technology and chief people officer for Forescout Technologies—said, "My parents never told me 'You could do whatever you wanted,' but they also never told me I couldn't do whatever I wanted to." Read that last sentence again but slower, and it will make sense.

Another person I spoke to who recently ran seven marathons in seven days on seven continents said, "I have ruled out winning Olympic gold in the hundred-meter sprint. I know my body and like to focus on realistic goals." While still young for many accomplishments, forty is a bit old to win an Olympic medal as a sprinter. Keep in mind, her definition of "realistic goals" involves running seven marathons in seven days on seven continents. We all view "realistic" differently. And realistically, you are probably not judging realistically correctly—it is likely a few steps further than you believe capable. I've seen this over and over in my own life and heard it consistently during my interviews.

We live in a day when our kids are taught that they cannot fail. Everyone gets a trophy. Everyone is a winner. Everyone is supposed to be great at everything. I wish this were the case, but it is just not true. I coached my son's soccer team, and we only won one game. We were not good. We did not deserve a trophy. Maybe it was the coach. Maybe it was the players. But with practice and hard work, we could get better. Maybe that is the mantra we should model for our kids instead of "Everyone's a winner." I also heard this theme over and over in my interviews.

> "My parents never told me 'You could do whatever you wanted,' but they also never told me I couldn't do whatever I wanted to."
>
> **Julie Cullivan**, former CIO of FireEye and CTO and CPO of Forescout Technologies

Choosing goals that are "realistic" is difficult because it is a relative term. Also, it means conceiving of far greater accomplishments than you may right now think are possible. My view and the view of so many I talked with is that, while we cannot do anything we want, we can do more than we can imagine. We tend to be more conservative about what we believe is "realistic." I think the army is more correct when they say, "Be all that you can be." However, you must realize that you CAN BE more.

HARNESSING A GROWTH MINDSET

Carol Dweck, PhD, is a world-renowned Stanford University psychologist who researches why people succeed and how they foster success. In the 1970s, Dweck studied how children cope with failure. Some saw failure as the end of the world, whereas others relished in it and grew. In her 2006 best-selling book *Mindset,* she outlines two distinct types of mindsets: fixed and growth. Much of her original work, while centered on education and sports training, now shows strong application in the workplace. The people I spoke with confirmed this.

A person with a **fixed mindset** believes their basic qualities such as intelligence and talent are fixed traits with which they were born. They are binary: you either have them or you do not. For example, some people are natural-born leaders, swimmers, or artists. Therefore, one's success is based on talent and not effort. Because you are not in control of your abilities, you rationalize your failures with "I'm just not good at that." If you fail and someone tries to give you feedback, you tend to be defensive and not find it helpful because there is nothing you can do about the situation.

On the other side of the spectrum are people with a **growth mindset**. These people believe they are in control of their abilities and that one's intelligence and talent can be grown and further developed. They believe that if you are not good at something, it is because you just have not done the work or put in the time to get good at it. So the increased effort will eventually lead to increased performance or ability. LeBron James, arguably the best basketball player in the world, sums it up: "It's always about growth mindset. It's the fact that you know that you can get better, even at our age, even with our accolades, even with what we've done in our careers. We still feel like we can improve."

Psychologist Anders Ericsson supports this belief. He has a PhD in psychology and is an expert in experts. That is, he studies how experts perform and practice in areas such as music, medicine, sports, and chess. He says we are all born with the same gift of being adaptable; with practice, we have the ability to improve over time. His research established the "10,000-hour rule," which was popularized by Malcolm Gladwell in his book *Outliers*. While much was made of the nice round number, Ericsson's larger point was that a lot of time spent in *deliberate* practice leads to mastery. He talks about how you can drastically grow and improve by having a goal, focusing on that goal, pushing yourself outside your comfort zone, and getting feedback from a coach. Dweck, Ericsson, and Gladwell all passionately believe you can improve over time, and being deliberate about your focus will optimize the time you spend to achieve your goal.

This was evident in conversations like the one I had with Julie Cullivan. Julie's background, if you look at her resume, is in sales operations, so one could question why a CEO would take a risk putting her in the role of overseeing all technology and all people. Most companies separate these into two positions, and those leaders would have grown up in their respective fields. But her true strengths are her ability to listen, learn, and implement. So when asked to take on the role of chief people officer, a person with a fixed mindset would say, "I've never done this, so I don't know how." Julie, having a growth mindset, thought, "I've never done this, but I can learn how." And she did.

So let's head toward the starting line and talk about what must happen first.

No Excuses

WE THINK OF A VARIETY OF REASONS why we "cannot" do something, but most, in my mind, are just excuses holding us back. When someone throws out an idea and you find yourself saying, "**Yes, but…**" followed by one of these excuses, be sure to test your assumptions and get to the root of why you are saying no. Be cognizant of when you hear yourself say, "Yes, but…" And when you hear those words, give yourself a few seconds to assess why and if your response is a valid reason or an excuse. This is about awareness and honesty with yourself. How many times have you said, "Yes, but…" so you didn't have to admit publicly your true doubts?

…I've never done that before.

Everything in life—yes, everything—would fall into this category. Think about it: walking, talking, giving a speech, starting your first job, balancing your checkbook. OK, some of you may have never balanced your checkbook, but there is still hope. So just because you have not done something before does not mean you cannot do it. It just means that you have not done it before.

When faced with a new challenge, I often hear five responses. I refer to these as the Phases of Optimism:

PHASES OF OPTIMISM

I CAN'T | CAN I? | I CAN'T YET | HOW CAN I? | HOW CAN I NOW?

Each time you move from one phase to the next, you are showing increased optimism in the possibility of starting something courageous.

"I've never done it before" separates two different types of people. One person thinks that because they have never done something before, they cannot do it now. They have a fixed mindset, according to Dweck. They are clearly on the far-left end, or the pessimistic side, of this scale. And they are right: they cannot do it. Before you can accomplish anything, you need the confidence, or some belief, that you will be successful. I am a pragmatist, so just because you have confidence does not mean you will be successful. But it is a significant step in the right direction.

The second person thinks they have never done it before and gets excited because it is a new challenge. They have a growth mindset. They continue moving through the phases. In many cases, they skip the first phase and sometimes the second.

When moving from "I can't" to "Can I?," you stop believing it is impossible and start believing it is possible. While that level of possibility may be small, it is still greater than before. More importantly, it is the difference between believing there is no chance you could do something to believing there is a chance, albeit minuscule.

In the movie *Dumb and Dumber*, Jim Carrey's bumbling character Lloyd is trying to capture the heart of Mary, a beautiful, wealthy woman played by Lauren Holly—or at least to get her to go out on a date with him. While gazing into her eyes and after asking her out and waiting for her reply, he says, "What are my chances?" She says, "Not good. Like 1 in a million." With complete optimism, he responds with a smile and says, "So you are telling me there is a chance!" In his view, "1 in a million" was still a chance because he looked at the 1 versus the 999,999.

Once you stop believing something is impossible, you start believing it is possible. The level of possibility goes up significantly when you say, "I can't, yet" because you recognize that, with some barriers removed, you could potentially achieve this dream someday. And then asking, "How can I?" has moved you completely into the realm of possibility, and you are ready to start planning—at which time you ask, "How can I now?"

ASK YOURSELF: WHAT COULD MOVE ME ONE STEP TO THE RIGHT ON THIS SCALE?

…We do not know anything about the space (market).

This is like the prior point of "I've never done it before." You can learn. From the time I started writing this book, when I could not tell you the difference between an agent, a publisher, and a publicist, to the time it reached you, I learned a lot. Many of the CEOs I spoke with did not know everything they needed to know before they started up or took over their company. They learned. You can too.

ASK YOURSELF: WHAT INFORMATION DO I NEED, AND WHERE CAN I GET IT?

…I do not have enough time.

We all have the same amount of time in the day, so I posit that it is not a time issue but a priority issue. How is it a busy CEO who gets home to cook dinner and put her kids to bed can get to the gym and you cannot? Even after the rebuttals of, "Well, she has a nanny or a staff" are heard, I still stay firm with my argument. If I said you would get $1 million if you woke up one hour earlier every day and worked out, would you make it happen? Or what if it would reduce your chance of a heart attack and give you a longer, healthier life?

Time is a finite resource, and how we use it determines where we put our priorities. I have coached many executives who have used this excuse with me, and it does not go far. It is all about where your priorities are, which is covered later in this book.

ASK YOURSELF: IN WHICH AREAS OF MY LIFE AM I SPENDING TIME THAT ARE LESS IMPORTANT THAN THIS GOAL?

…I don't have enough money.

Unlike time, we all have different amounts of money. But like time, it is still about priorities. Save more, spend less. You may not have enough money today but when will you, and what do you have to give up to reach your dream?

ASK YOURSELF: WHERE CAN I REDUCE MY CURRENT SPENDING OR INCREASE MY CURRENT REVENUE TO FUND THIS INITIATIVE?

…I could fail.

That is correct; you could. And if you do fail, what could you lose? In some cases, it could be a loss of money. It could be a loss of time. Or it could be a loss of ego. Most people I spoke with, including myself, had failures, but it did not prevent them from trying again. They learned from the first time, improvised, and tried again. Some people started up companies and invested millions of dollars of their own or of others. And the company went under. They learned what went wrong and avoided it the next time. I had heard a story about an employee who made a very costly mistake for his company, and—thinking he was going to be fired—he approached the CEO. He apologized for his half-million-dollar mistake. After he said that he learned what he would do differently, he asked if he was going to be fired. The CEO responded, "I just invested half a million dollars in training you; I'd be a fool to fire you."

ASK YOURSELF: REALISTICALLY, WHAT IS THE WORST THING THAT COULD HAPPEN IF I FAIL?

...I am afraid.

Fear is a real reason to make you think, but not stop. Fear is a psychological barrier that we often overemphasize when the risk is actually low. As a psychotherapist, Jonathan Alpert, in his book *Be Fearless* writes, "You fear what you don't know." Fear is about uncertainty or "an inability to predict the future."[3] Alpert then goes on and writes, "You overcome fear not by avoiding it, but by facing it. The more you face your fear, the more fearless you will become."[4] It is one thing to be afraid of risking your life or your life savings, but most activities are not in those categories.

ASK YOURSELF: WHAT AM I AFRAID OF, AND HOW CAN I REDUCE MY FEAR?

...It is too much risk.

We are starting to move from excuses to legitimate reasons for not doing something. I get this. We may need to assess the situation more. But make sure you are assessing the risk of something happening versus your fear of an event. Risk generally assumes a statistical probability the event will happen, where fear is more psychological, involving your perception and feelings about the risk.

Shortly before my first child was born, I was out on a bike ride. As I started to descend this long, steep hill, one on which I would normally reach at least forty-five mph, I thought for a moment. It was early in the morning, and the roads were a bit damp from the dew. If I crash, it is not just my life I am jeopardizing but my soon-to-be-born son's. He needs a father. I gently squeezed on the brakes and slowed to a more reasonable thirty-five mph. But I still went down the hill.

Is there a way to mitigate the risk? Because in many things you do, you could get hurt. You could be hurt emotionally (striking up a conversation with that person across the room who has caught your eye), financially (investing in a new business), or even physically (breaking a leg as you do a more advanced ski run). Think about it, you could get hurt driving to work, but that does not stop you. You take precautions to reduce the risk.

Many people who are afraid to fly think flying is too risky. What they don't realize is that they are at more risk driving to the airport than flying on the airplane. According to the ICAO (United Nations' International Civil Aviation Organization), there were zero fatalities on commercial flights within the United States between 2014 and 2017. Between 2008 and 2018, there were sixty fatalities (2009 had fifty fatalities).[5] According to a National Safety Council (NSC) article titled "Protect Yourself and Loved Ones by Addressing Roadway Risks," there were an estimated forty-two thousand people killed in motor vehicle crashes in 2020.[6] The article states, "Our roadways continue to pose some of the biggest risks we face each day." So it may seem it is safer to fly to your destination than to drive to the airport.

Heck, your chances of dying in your lifetime in a motor vehicle crash are 1:107 compared to being stung by a hornet, wasp, or bee at 1:59,507.[7] So it is safer to be eating your burger and watermelon with the bees than driving to the picnic. But it is the bee that scares us.

Despite the statistics, we still drive. We still put ourselves at risk every day. But we also look at ways to mitigate those risks. We buy cars with airbags, drive more cautiously, avoid driving after drinking alcohol, and wear seat belts.

ASK YOURSELF: WHAT SEAT BELTS EXIST FOR MY DREAM, AND HOW CAN I REDUCE ANY RISK?

...I don't want to.

This is one of the few responses that makes sense to me. If you do not have the desire, then move on to other endeavors. To do something requires 1) resources (time and money); 2) know-how (skills and knowledge); and 3) desire. The first two are easier to come by than the last one. I have a close friend who is an excellent writer, has published numerous newspaper articles, and teaches college English. He has the resources and know-how to write a book. He can tell a remarkable story. However, he does not have the desire. End of story.

This is what often differentiates "I can't" versus "I shouldn't."

"I can't…" refers to resources or know-how.

> ﹥ I can't get the funding.
> ﹥ I can't find the time.
> ﹥ I can't figure out where to start.
> ﹥ I can't learn how to […].

"I shouldn't…" refers to desire.

> ﹥ I shouldn't take on this project, as it would require too much time away from my family, and I just don't want to do that right now.
> ﹥ I shouldn't take on this project because it is not aligned with our business plans.
> ﹥ I shouldn't start this new idea, as it would put our financial plan at more risk than I would feel comfortable with at this time.
> ﹥ I shouldn't start this project because it does not align with my longer-term goals.

ASK YOURSELF: ON A SCALE OF 1 TO 10, HOW BADLY DO I WANT THIS?

So when evaluating if you should pursue a big idea, consider what is stopping you. Resources and know-how can be obtained. It may not be easy, but it is doable.

FAILURE IS AN OPTION

Are you failing? I skied a lot as a kid, and every winter my parents would take us out of school for a week-long ski trip. After a long day on the slopes in Breckenridge, Colorado, I skied down and glided in next to my dad. With the confidence of an elite ski racer and feeling proud, I said to him, "I haven't fallen all day." My dad then complimented me on my form and then quietly asked, "Did you push yourself hard enough today?" I then realized that falling is not failing; it is growing. I fell a few times the next day. And while people may tell you failing is good, I would rather not. But when I do, I will learn how to avoid it the next time.

However, sometimes failure is not an option. Most of us are not trying to retrieve three stranded astronauts from a potentially fatal space mission like Apollo 13's successful failure. When NASA Flight Director Gene Kranz said, "Failure is not an option," he wanted to avoid three astronauts losing their lives. Few of us, however, are in those shoes.

Most of us are not putting our life savings at risk, although some of the people I spoke with did. We are trying to finish a big race, implement a major project at work, get a much-deserved promotion, start a company, travel around the world, pivot a company, or accomplish some lifelong dream. In most cases, lives are not at stake. The risk of failing often means losing money, wasting time, or crushing your ego. But you will survive.

We all have failures, but those who see the failure as next week's challenge are the people who go further. Consider a few notable ones. Steve Jobs founded Apple Computer in 1976 and was fired in 1985 after a dispute with the board of directors. Jobs left and founded another computer company. Ironically, he sold that company to Apple in 1997 after Apple went through several CEOs. Steve Jobs was eventually rehired into his old job and took the company further than anyone could have imagined. In 2018, Apple Computer became the first trillion-dollar company thanks in large part to Jobs's ability to see the future and invent products most customers never knew they needed.

James Dyson, in his attempt to make a better vacuum, made 5,126 that sucked (figuratively) until his 5,127th prototype sucked more (literally) than all the ones before it.[8] He never gave up. When I asked Shane Kenny—a serial entrepreneur who sold his first startup to McAfee for a nice profit—what mistake people make most often, he said: "Most people fail right before they were to succeed because they just gave up." A person's willingness to complete amazing things often is not about their willingness to keep going but their fortitude to not stop.

It took the company that created the popular degreaser WD-40 thirty-nine previous tries before turning out a product that worked.[9] It is aptly named because on the fortieth attempt, scientists arrived at the perfect solution.

Sometimes failure turns into something positive. Fred Kitson led a team that turned a failure into a big success. A former executive for HP and Motorola, he now advises companies on how to turn the "extremely technical and somewhat complicated world of computers…to 'simple-to-use consumer products.'" He shared with me how what initially was seen as a failed product actually turned out to be a big win for his company. In 1997 while at HP, he was asked to build a handheld scanner. It failed as a scanner, but they repackaged the key sensor chip, creating the opportunity to make a really good mouse. HP sold those scanner capabilities to Microsoft in 1999, which became the basis for the MS "Intellimouse." Within just a few years, all computer mice went from the "roller balls," which collected dirt and grime, to more effective "optical sensors." Chances are that the mouse you use at your computer is a result of this "failure."

Failure is not ideal, but it is often a reality and a possibility. It should, however, not be the starting place. While reading a cycling blog, I learned of a woman who wanted to ride her bicycle five hundred miles. She started not sure she could go that far but felt confident she could make it three hundred miles. Coincidentally, or likely not, she quit just past three hundred miles. Riding five hundred miles is hard—I know because I rode four thousand miles across the United States. But she quit before she even started. If you do not think you can reach the finish line before you get to the starting line, you are probably right.

However, when you have never done something before, it may be hard to have the confidence that you can do it the first time. The people I spoke with had many things in common, and confidence was one. They knew it would not be easy. They knew there would be missteps along the way. But they also knew they would figure out how to keep going. As several entrepreneurs said, "I am 100 percent comfortable betting on myself."

Kevin Chou, founder of several online gaming and eSports companies, said about failure, "It almost doesn't enter my head to not think about going forward. I may ultimately fail, and I am OK with that. I am more at peace than if I tried and failed. This helped me not worry about it much. If I made all my decisions to prevent failure, then I would do things differently. I envision what success could look like. I envision what failure looks like and emotionally imagine what it would be like and make peace with that."

Successful people know that failure is an option because most have had some doozies. But they start with the confidence that the outcome is very realistic and likely will be accomplished.

There are a lot of people who will tell you "No" or "You can't" or "You shouldn't." But do not let it be you. Oprah Winfrey was told she "wasn't fit for TV," Walt Disney was told he "lacked imagination," and Anna Wintour, famed editor-in-chief for *Vogue*, was fired for being "a little too edgy."[10] The Beatles were told they have "no future in show business."[11] They seemed to have done all right. Just because someone tells you it cannot be done does not mean you should not pursue it. It means THEY don't think it can be done.

More importantly, what do you think?

WHEN THE CHANCE OF FAILURE IS HIGH, THE RISK OF FAILING IS LOW

Several years into my career, I was asked to lead a major change management initiative on a project that had failed twice before. It was the largest financial database conversion the company had gone through and one of the largest in the financial services industry. The senior management team decided to bring in an outside project manager who had previously run similar conversions. But people were still skeptical. I was then asked to take the lead in training several thousand people on this unknown system that few wanted. I was given the option to lead the project or pass it on to someone else.

Why would I risk taking on an initiative that had failed twice before when a highly visible failure could be career suicide? I realized the company had learned from its past two failures, and they were bringing on a project manager with more experience, authority, and access to the CEO than the previous two times. After I asked, I too was given more authority and access than my two predecessors. I was surrounded by people who wanted me to succeed and would do almost anything to make sure the third time was the charm. But even if the project failed, I did not feel I had much to lose because other people had not accomplished the task either. When I was given the opportunity to lead this effort, it was an easy decision.

While the project ended up costing more than initially projected (don't most?) and taking slightly more time than estimated (again, don't most?), it was deemed one of the biggest operational successes the company had achieved. We reached our goals of migrating millions of data elements from one system to another and making sure all the employees knew how to use the new system. While the chance of failure was high, I felt the risk to me personally was low.

Now that you have gotten the excuses out of the way and realized that failure is not the end of the world, it's time to envision what is possible and turn your dreams into reality.

PILLAR I – ENVISION

"If we did all the things we are capable of, we would literally astound ourselves."
Thomas Edison, inventor

ENVISION

your big ideas and goals in all the important areas of your life: career, relationships, hobbies, health, fitness, finances—you name it. This is about understanding what is important to you long term and identifying the more substantial dreams you want to accomplish. It is about being more deliberate with your actions so as you get older you have few regrets.

SYNONYMS

DREAM

VISION

CONCEPTUALIZE

THINK BIG

PURPOSE

A CRUCIAL ELEMENT OF achieving greatness is seeing greatness. It is about visualizing what the finish line looks and feels like well before starting. It is about looking years out and striving for goals that align with your long-term vision and your values. I started running later in life, with my first goal being to finish a marathon. At that time, I did not know about the two-hundred-mile run, so it was not part of my long-term goal. However, staying in decent shape and having something to focus on has always been part of who I am.

So when I heard of the Tahoe 200, it appealed to me. I wrote the idea down where I keep a list of other thoughts. Some of those continually creep back into my head over time, which serves as a sign to me.

If over time an idea keeps coming back into your mind, it may be time to explore its possibilities. This one didn't stay on the list very long because I kept thinking about how cool it would be to run around one of the most beautiful lakes in the world and how I would feel at the end. You may be thinking, "You are going to feel like crap—in great pain, hungry, and tired, and be filthy." Yep, all true, but I kept thinking about how rewarding it would be to cross the finish line with my hands in the air, screaming and crying for joy while being embraced by my wife. For over a year, that image rarely left my head. For any big accomplishment, the emotion of finishing must be more profound than the pain and suffering you will experience during the adventure. This is your emotional journey.

THE FINE LINE BETWEEN CRAZY AND COURAGEOUS

How do you know if your idea is crazy or if you are being courageous? I attempted to find out by asking everyone I interviewed that question and trying to understand the difference. In 1962, I am sure many people asked that same question of JFK when he said . . .

We choose to go to the moon! We choose to go to the moon in this decade and do the other things, not because they are easy, but because they are hard; because that goal will serve to organize and measure the best of our energies and skills, because that challenge is one that we are willing to accept, one we are unwilling to postpone, and one we intend to win, and the others, too.

I believe that this nation should commit itself to achieving the goal, before this decade is out, of landing a man on the moon and returning him safely to the earth.

Landing a man on the moon is often the benchmark for unimaginable ideas. How many times have you heard, "If we can land a man on the moon, we can surely do _____?" This has always been the greatest rebuttal to anyone thinking something was too big. I am guessing those people hate Neil Armstrong.

So how do you know you are thinking big enough? Most of the people I spoke with never considered their ideas crazy.

Mark Lewis, former CEO of Violin Systems, entrepreneur, and venture capitalist summed it up best: "I think the main difference between crazy and courageous is whether you are successful or not. We never hear about the one thousand failures but always about the success. All of these ideas are crazy until they are not."

> "I think the main difference between crazy and courageous is whether you are successful or not."
>
> **Mark Lewis**, former CEO, entrepreneur, venture capitalist, and board member for several technology companies

Entrepreneur Jordan Epstein, who started up a company to revolutionize health care costs, said, "Looking back, it was closer to the crazy side." He saw a problem that doctors continually struggle to answer: the simple question of how much a procedure would cost, and then if that cost was worth it. Jordan told me it was the biggest professional risk he has taken and required him to leave a solid job with a salary and benefits and live in his parents' basement.

In what is the mantra of so many successful people, Jordan said, "I believed I could do it. I believed it was possible." The common thread among most of the people I spoke with is that they had the confidence in themselves and believed in their idea and did not think it was crazy.

Mark Friedman took on one of the more challenging projects of his life. As a real estate developer and active community member, he led a group to develop the Golden 1 Center where the Sacramento Kings play basketball. The Kings played in an outdated stadium on the outskirts of town, and they wanted to bring something closer to the heart of the city and revitalize downtown. He told me, "I remember when the arena was being started and how daunting it seemed. I had confidence that I would figure it out along the way. I didn't know how we were going to get there, but I didn't doubt we would. Building an arena was way outside my wheelhouse, but I realized that I could bring people to the table." About a year after my conversation with Mark, I was invited to the arena to watch the Kings play, and it was quite an impressive building. His confidence paid off.

Diann Boyle, a former air force pilot, shared a story with me about how her son was working toward his pilot's license. Having just completed his first year at the Air Force Academy, he wanted to get his pilot's license during his summer break. His mom, an Air Force Academy graduate and retired commercial pilot, and his father, also a commercial pilot, understood what it takes. So when her son asked, "Mom, do you think I could get my private pilot's license by the end of the summer?"

while she knew he could do it, she posed the following back to him—
"The real question is, do you?"

Confidence, however, does not come overnight. It comes from a smaller success, which becomes a bigger success, which become an even bigger success. And it comes with some failures in between.

Jordan's first attempt to solve this problem did not work as he planned. He told me, "The reason it hasn't been done is not that it is impossible but because it is hard." He is one of the smarter guys I know, and when this problem is eventually solved, I am betting he will be part of it. People who accomplish extraordinary things in life do not let one failure stop them. They see that one failure as another roadblock they need to go around.

Granted, some ideas may be just too big for you at this point in your life. As I mentioned earlier, I have ruled out winning, or even riding in, the Tour de France. Others have ruled out winning the Boston Marathon or being a runway model in New York City or starting their own business. But they, and I, ruled that out based on statistics that were compelling enough to focus our energy in this area. There are anomalies, but we must weigh the chance of success versus the commitment needed and then ask if that resource commitment should be used for other ventures.

BEHAVIORS (ENVISION)

The EPIC framework consists of five pillars, and each pillar has three behaviors. The Envision pillar is broken into these three behaviors:

1 **Define your purpose**: I have a clear vision of what I want to accomplish long term, and my shorter-term goals move me in that direction.

2 **Stretch yourself**: I purposely push myself into opportunities that make me uncomfortable and test myself in new areas.

3 **Hone your dream bigger strategy**: I deliberately think of ways to stretch myself and explore what could be possible over a long time frame.

Chapter 1

DEFINE YOUR PURPOSE

> "Twenty years from now you will be more disap-
> pointed by the things that you didn't do than by
> the ones you did do. So, throw off the bowlines.
> Sail away from the safe harbor. Catch the trade
> winds in your sails. Explore. Dream. Discover."
> **Mark Twain,** writer

WHEN I WAS TWENTY-ONE YEARS OLD, I went through Stephen Covey's "7 Habits of Highly Successful People" program. My college profes-sor used the material as part of a management class and knew Stephen Covey. So he invited him to be a guest lecturer one day. It was shortly after the book was published and before it became a bestseller, so none of us knew who this very charismatic bald guy from Utah was. We would soon learn. During that class, I wrote down a series of values or areas that were important to me. Over the years I have refined them a little, but the core of what I wrote then is still true today. It helped me define what was important to me and WHY.

FIND YOUR WHY

During our lifetime, we can all change the world. In some cases, it is a profound impact on humanity such as the work of Mother Teresa, Mahatma Gandhi, or Bill Gates. In other cases, it is my fourth-grade teacher, who impacted the lives of twenty-five children every year for thirty years, or my uncle, who tirelessly raised money to take thousands of wheelchairs down to needy individuals in developing nations. I think of a friend who started a foundation to raise money for local schools many years ago that now contributes over $600,000 a year to educational programs. While some may have had millions of people supporting their cause or billions of dollars to impact change, most of us do not. However, all these people had a purpose and stayed focused to accomplish that purpose. They had their WHY.

The most common thread I heard during my interviews was that most were clear on why they were trying to accomplish their goal and focused their time and energy around achieving that goal. They thought big and stayed focused.

Barry Broome is the CEO of the Greater Sacramento Economic Council, which is the economic development engine for Sacramento and the surrounding area. The region consists of twenty cities, towns, and counties with about two and a half million people and is often seen as the stepchild of the San Francisco Bay Area. As the state capital for California, which has the fifth-largest economy in the world, Sacramento lags behind so many cities its size in economic measures. Barry, after turning other economies around, was hired to bring life to this region and turn it into a leader.

Having consulted with his organization for many years, I have come to know Barry well. He is wicked smart. He has courageously grandiose ideas. He has a seemingly endless supply of energy. Barry sees his role as changing the world and often says, "If you can change Sacramento, you can change California. If you change California, you change America. And if you change the America, you change the world." He thinks big.

When I asked him how he does it, he told me that there must be a lot of emotion tied to your vision. He went on to tell me a very heartfelt story about how his dad lost his job when Barry was sixteen. His dad never got another job and lost his dignity. In many cases, a man's life is measured by his career, and his yardstick just broke.

Barry saw the impact it had on his father and never wanted either himself or others to feel the same. So he has focused his career on turning economies around. For Barry, turning the Sacramento region into a booming economy is not just a job; it is a deeply held emotional goal so other parents do not experience what his father did. He talked about how his vision has made a profound impact and that he isolates his body of work around profound impacts. To Barry, his WHY is clear.

In 1988, Albert Dyrness founded Advent Engineering Services and grew it to 130 people. He told me how that same drive and passion that allowed him success in business bled into his personal life as well. During a routine physical, his doctor told him he needed to lose some weight. It is a battle many people deal with every day, but Albert had his WHY, as he told me. He believed that his grandfather died of a bad back because the pain kept him confined to a couch. The sedentary lifestyle eventually took over, and Albert did not want that to happen to him. Albert did "get off the couch" and started to bike and swim. Eventually, he went on to finish his first Ironman, which is a one-day event consisting of a 2.4-mile swim, 112-mile bike ride, and 26.2-mile run. During the difficult days in the pool, on the bike, or at the gym, he would always think of why he was out there. He did not want to die on the couch like his grandpa. Albert had his WHY.

But not all are tied so closely to one's family.

For Alicia Wallace of All Across Africa, her benefits were seeing the lives of thousands of African women being improved. She is an extremely bright woman and could easily find another job if her company went out of business. And she would easily double or triple her salary. In 2009 on a medical mission in Sierra Leone, she saw crushing poverty and said to herself that she needed to do something to help solve the problem. At age twenty-two she decided to do something in that space. With a billion people in Africa and 80 percent in poverty, Alicia set out to make a difference.

She has created a business through which thousands of women in Rwanda see their income increase four times by weaving beautiful, hand-crafted baskets. I was fortunate to be in Rwanda when All Across Africa conducted its annual celebration, in which over two thousand women came together in one place to celebrate the year's accomplishments. Their lives are vastly improved because Alicia and her cofounder Greg Stone have found their WHY and are truly making a difference in the world.

All four of these people are emotionally tied to their goals. Their WHY has such a strong emotional payoff that it keeps them going during the difficult times. It provides clarity in their life.

Ask yourself if you are emotionally tied to your goal and what that emotional payoff will be when you reach the end. This will help you out of the trough of despair. These benefits come in many forms, including emotional, physical, financial, and career. I am sure you can add even more payoffs to this list.

I stood at the finish line as a friend completed a fifty-mile run. When he ran through the finisher's arch, he started to cry—not because he was disappointed by his time or in great pain but because he was happy with his accomplishment. Don't get me wrong, he WAS in great pain. But finishing a fifty-mile run is emotional because of how proud you feel to have accomplished something many do not even dream of. When was the last time you cried because you were thrilled with what you finished? If your feeling of elation at the finish line is greater than your feeling of deflation along the journey, seriously consider taking the journey. You may not regret it.

LIVE LIKE YOU WERE DYING

Imagine you were eighty, and the end was within sight. What would you regret?

Bronnie Ware spent eight years as a caregiver for people who were in their last three to twelve weeks of life. They knew they were dying, and Ware would sit and listen to what her patients said. What stood out was how many of them had regrets. In her book, *The Top Five Regrets of the Dying: A Life Transformed by the Dearly Departing*, Ware talks about what people most regretted. Most regrets dealt with a lack of courage.

Most wish they had more courage to live a life true to themselves versus what others expected. They realized that many dreams had gone unfulfilled and that they had not accomplished even half of their dreams.[12]

This is also backed up by a study of two thousand adults out of Britain by UK nonprofit Remember A Charity, which asked people how they feel about their life choices.

> Four out of ten people regret how they have lived their lives so far. Spending too much time at work and not traveling enough were among respondents' biggest regrets. Other common regrets among those surveyed included neglecting their health and not spending enough time with their family. Close to half of those surveyed said they regret focusing so much on financial success as opposed to more meaningful endeavors.

Many believe all hope is not lost; more than half of respondents say that they know it's not too late for them to change paths and accomplish more in life. Inaction seems to be the biggest cause of regret, with three in four adults claiming that their regret is mainly caused by things they wanted to do but never got around to.[13]

In summary, we more often regret what we didn't do versus what we did do.

Jeff Bezos, the founder of Amazon.com, recognized this issue as he was trying to decide if he should leave a solid job and pursue a crazy idea to create an online book retailer. He used his "Regret Minimization Framework" to help him decide. It is a basic model asking one question: "In X years, will I regret not doing this? If the answer is 'no' then don't bother. If the answer is 'yes' then do it." He goes on to explain:

> I wanted to project myself forward to age 80 and say, "Okay, now I'm looking back on my life. I want to have minimized the number of regrets I have." I knew that when I was 80, I was not going to regret having tried this. I was not going to regret trying to participate in this thing called the Internet that I thought was going to be a really big deal. I knew that if I failed, I wouldn't regret that, but I knew the one thing I might regret is not ever having tried. I knew that that would haunt me every day, and so when I thought about it that way it was an incredibly easy decision.[14]

The irony of Bezos's framework is how simple it is. Having founded a company that has conquered the world with data, complex algorithms, analysis, and more data, you would have thought his decision-making framework would be more robust. But it isn't. I am a strong proponent of using data to measure risk, analyze progress, and determine success, and we will talk about that later, but I love the simplicity of this model. Try it next time you are thinking of something bold.

While unaware of Bezos's framework at the time, I have used the same concept. Shortly after I met my wife, I shared with her my goal of traveling around the world. I was thirty-seven years old and in the prime of my career. The work was exciting and challenging, most of my colleagues were great to work with, my boss gave me freedom and mentoring, and I was making more money than I needed. But that 1,300-person company had just been acquired by a 30,000-person behemoth based on the other side of the country. Having been through many acquisitions, I expected all this would change as the top-notch leadership I was accustomed to would leave, and all decisions would move to a new headquarters.

I had to decide to focus on my career—either with the new company or look for a new opportunity—or travel around the world. The answer came quite quickly and easily when I asked myself, "In twenty years, will I regret not taking seven months off and traveling around the world with this beautiful woman?" Since we were not married and did not have kids, now was the time because it was going to be too difficult later in life. So I thought.

Twelve years after that once-in-a-lifetime adventure and with nine- and eleven-year-old boys, my wife and I were preparing for our second trip around the world. "Would we regret not taking our kids out of school for one year and traveling around the world?" Again, the answer came quickly and easily, as we did not want to miss out on the bond we would build with our children and the opportunity for them to be global citizens. Like the first trip around the world, I figured we could always come home if things were not going well. To this day, I have never regretted taking either of those adventures. But I do feel confident I would have regret had I chosen not to go.

David Alonso, an institutional investor I spoke to, asked similar questions when he was thinking of leaving his successful career so his wife and three daughters could spend one year traveling the world. For him it was easy because he too did not want to look back in twenty years when his girls had moved out of the house and were focusing on their own lives and think, "I wish we would have spent that year traveling."

I have tried to live my life so that if I died today, I would have lived a fulfilling life of someone my age. Coincidentally, the second regret Ware talks about is that people say they "wish they hadn't worked so hard."[15] However, accomplishing big dreams does not come easy and requires a lot of hard work.

DECIDE WHERE YOU WANT TO BE IN TEN YEARS

Big ideas are not implemented overnight. It took seven years from the time John F. Kennedy said we would send a man to the moon to when we did. And that was quick. In today's fast-paced, "get rich quick" world, we must realize that big things take time. The entrepreneurs I interviewed said they are thinking beyond the next technologies since someone is already working on the "next" technology. Their brains are sometimes decades ahead of today.

John Newton, who cofounded the software company Documentum, which was later sold to EMC for $1.7 billion, says, "I am always thinking ten years out, and every five years, I extrapolate out trends in technology to see what could be next." He says that he can predict what technologies can do in five to ten years using concepts like Moore's Law, which says processing power will double every two years. The adoption of new technology and ideas is accelerating at a rapid pace. According to a 2019 *Harvard Business Review* article, "The Pace of Technology Adoption Is Speeding Up":

An automobile industry trade consultant, for instance, observes that, "Today, a typical automotive design cycle is approximately 24 to 36 months, which is much faster than the 60-month life cycle from five years ago." . . . It took decades for the telephone to reach 50% of households, beginning before 1900. It took five years or less for cellphones to accomplish the same penetration in 1990.[16]

Because of these rapid changes, one must be able to think outside the box to understand how the future will look. We may not be able to see the future, but we can make informed guesses about what it may bring.

The roots of John's company started when he was an undergraduate at the University of California, Berkeley, in 1976. Relational databases were a new concept, and the courses he took on the subject appealed to him. There were no tools at the time to make a better database, and he thought he could change that. He then started to ruminate on the concept that eventually became the billion-dollar idea.

A shared trait that John and so many successful executives have is that they are deliberate in how they spend their time, money, energy, and processing power. John saw a problem and knew he could build a better solution. So many people— not the ones I interviewed—say, "I will let fate decide where I will be in

> "I am always thinking ten years out, and every five years, I extrapolate out trends in technology to see what could be next."
>
> **John Newton,** cofounder of the software company Documentum and chief strategy officer and board member for several technology companies

ten years." They will get somewhere. It just may not be where they would have chosen to go. But the people I interviewed decided where they wanted to be and then focused on getting there. Would you want your pilot to take off and fly where the wind took her or fly directly to your preferred destination?

In a CNN Business interview, Sheryl Sandburg, chief operating officer for Facebook, was asked what she wished she had learned early in her career. "You don't have to have it all figured out," she said. "But I do think you can have two goals at once: a long-term dream and a short-term plan. Set personal goals for what you want to do in the future and what you want to learn in the next year-and-a-half. Ask yourself how you can improve and what you're afraid to do—that's usually the thing you should try."

ACTIVITIES

QUESTIONS TO ASK YOURSELF

> What is most important in your life?
> What are your four to six core values?
> Are you living up to those values?
> What is on your bucket list?
> What would you want to have accomplished in five, ten, twenty, or thirty years?
> Is there anything you will regret not doing when you are eighty?
> What big idea comes back into your head from time to time?
> What is one dream you want to accomplish?
> Where do you want to make a difference in the world?

EXERCISES

> Write down a list of one hundred things you want to do before you are eighty.
> Choose five items from that list that really get you excited.
> Choose at least one item and write the payoff (emotional, physical, financial, career, etc.) you will get when you are done.
> Write down the eulogy you would want read at your funeral.
> Write a press release as if you were announcing your accomplishment to the newspaper.

Chapter 2

STRETCH YOURSELF

> "If you want something you've never had, you must be willing to do something you've never done."
> **Thomas Jefferson,** United States president

MOST BIG GOALS involve challenging work and a lot of pain and suffering. You will, at times, question your sanity and wonder what the hell you are doing. At some points you will be so excited you cannot stop working on it, and other times you will be frustrated beyond belief. Pushing yourself into new territories allows you to grow. But it can be scary.

We all get scared. Barbra Streisand gets stage fright because she does not want to disappoint her audience. Famed Oakland Raiders football coach John Madden was afraid to fly and used a bus to get around the country. Michael Jackson also had a fear of flying. While most of us do not have such extreme phobias that could impact our career, we do get nervous, feel anxious, and have fears. These prevent us from going further and exploring new territories. And while doing something new can be scary, it can also be exciting.

FACE YOUR FEARS

Whether those nerves scare you or excite you is a significant factor in determining your success. According to psychotherapist Jonathan Alpert, "Fear and excitement are physiologically similar. The difference is not how your body feels but rather how your mind interprets it. When you tell yourself you are suffering from nerves, you reinforce the fear and end up having a negative experience. When you tell yourself you are excited, you weaken the fear and turn what could have been a negative into a positive."[17] Both are a state of arousal with increased heart rate, butterflies in the stomach, sweaty palms, or nervousness. Think of riding a roller coaster. We ride these because they give us a thrill and make us feel like we are in real danger. Realistically, the danger factor is low. According to the International Association of Amusement Parks & Attractions, your chances of injury are one in 24 million and being killed is one in 750 million. So at the fair, it is the corn dog that will kill you—not the roller coaster.

Fear is a good thing. It has kept our species from going extinct. When early man would be out hunting and come across a deadly predator, the fear would cause him to back away (flight). Or, if charged, he would attack (fight). Those fight or flight instincts are a protective measure to keep us alive. However, sometimes fear impacts you moving forward even when the danger level is low. Whether the fear is real or just fabricated in our minds, it still stops us in our tracks or significantly slows us down. Fear is what defines each person's boundaries, so the more we can reduce our fear, the wider our boundaries can go. What are you most afraid will happen?

1. **Losing money.** The market takes a dive and significantly impacts your investments, or a major customer leaves, and revenue does not materialize as expected. You are afraid you won't be able to pay the bills.

2. **Impacting career.** You do not reach the expectations of your boss or the people around you because you went out on a limb and fell. You are afraid they will look at you negatively.

3. **Getting physically injured.** You fall and break a bone or stress your body beyond its physical limit. You are afraid of the pain.

4. **Becoming psychologically hurt.** The self-fulfilling prophecy of "This is too big" kicks in, and you start to feel despair, sadness, complacency, or anger. This could emotionally scar you from trying something big again. You are afraid to fail.

These, and so many others, are all very real fears and possible outcomes. But as psychologist and author John Schinnerer, PhD, told me, "Fear and doubt kill more dreams than failure ever has." John knows this subject well. He was a consultant to Pixar's Academy Award–winning movie *Inside Out*, where the main character, named Riley, learns to deal with her emotions, including fear. Many leaders I spoke to reiterate this concept and said that too often we are held back by fear.

I get it. Fear has definitely held me back. I was afraid to fail in my career and avoided taking bigger leaps. I was afraid to ask the pretty girl across the room out because I figured she would say no. And she did many times. I do not like riding up glass elevators in tall buildings. So the trip to the top of the Eiffel Tower when the elevator ascends makes me nervous. But the view at the top is beautiful, and

> "Fear and doubt kill more dreams than failure ever has."
>
> **John Schinnerer,** PhD, psychologist, and consultant to Academy Award-winning movie *Inside Out*

thousands of people survive it every day. If that fear stopped me in my tracks, I would never see the Champs-Élysées or the Seine or the Arc de Triomphe from nine hundred feet above. Facing fears is tough, but it can open up rewarding views and possibilities.

Facing these fears, or exposure therapy, is an effective way to address the issue. According to the American Psychological Association (APA):

> Exposure Therapy is a psychological treatment that was developed to help people confront their fears. When people are fearful of something, they tend to avoid the feared objects, activities, or situations. Although this avoidance might help reduce feelings of fear in the short term, over the long term it can make the fear become even worse. In such situations, a psychologist might recommend a program of exposure therapy in order to help break the pattern of avoidance and fear. In this form of therapy, psychologists create a safe environment in which to "expose" individuals to the things they fear and avoid. The exposure to the feared objects, activities or situations in a safe environment helps reduce fear and decrease avoidance.[18]

The APA outlines four types of exposure therapy:[19]

1. **In vivo exposure:** Directly facing a feared object, situation, or activity in real life. For example, someone with a fear of snakes might be instructed to handle a snake, or someone with social anxiety might be instructed to give a speech in front of an audience.

2. **Imaginal exposure:** Vividly imagining the feared object, situation, or activity. For example, someone with post-traumatic stress disorder might be asked to recall and describe his or her traumatic experience to reduce feelings of fear.

3. **Virtual reality exposure:** In some cases, virtual reality technology can be used when in vivo exposure is not practical. For example, someone with a fear of flying might take a virtual flight in the psychologist's office, using equipment that provides the sights, sounds, and smells of an airplane.

4. **Interoceptive exposure:** Deliberately bringing on physical sensations that are harmless yet feared. For example, someone with panic disorder might be instructed to run in place to make his or her heart speed up, and therefore learn that this sensation is not dangerous.

Fear is normal. Whether you are nervous about the swim portion of an Ironman, presenting your business plan to venture capitalists, or starting up a new project at work, exposing yourself to smaller versions of your idea will build your comfort and confidence and allow you to take on even more.

Having success in one area can lead to success in another area. Another way to do this is by starting small and building up to your ultimate goal.

While I will focus more on this topic under Plan and Iterate, it is a critical element to stretching yourself. I'll reiterate what Barry Broome says: "If you can change Sacramento, you can change California. If you can change California, you can change America. And if you can change America, you can change the world." One could argue that his starting place is fairly large, but not on a relative scale. This is similar to exposure therapy and what psychologist Jonathan Alpert addresses in his book, *Be Fearless.* If you are deathly afraid of snakes, do not get into a room with a black mamba. Start with a baby garter snake. Look at it while it is in its terrarium, then maybe stick your hand in and touch it, then pet it, then pick it up, then…. Now do the same with giving a presentation. Practice it in your own room and then in front of a few people, and then more people, and then…. Or with running a marathon. Start running 1 mile, then 2, and then 26.2. Small things are not nearly as intimidating and are much easier to bite off than their larger counterparts.

IF IT MAKES YOUR PALMS SWEAT, DO IT

While you may be hesitant to start something you are afraid of, pick something that makes your palms sweat. Choosing something that scares you puts you well outside the comfort zone, but choosing something that makes you nervous is very manageable. It is normal to be nervous. It's good to be nervous.

I have coached many executives who have confided in me that they get butterflies in their stomach before a big presentation. These are people who routinely talk in front of hundreds or thousands of people.

Erik Molitor, CIO for Bio-Rad Laboratories, looks for things that make his palms sweat: "It forces me out of my comfort zone to gain experience. At some points, this has probably led to a few gray hairs and sleepless nights when I've bitten off more than I can chew, but I'm also sure it's what has led me to reach my goal." Later in the book, under Iterate, we'll learn what Erik's goal was.

The more times you put yourself in these uncomfortable situations, the more you get comfortable being uncomfortable. Dave Osh has been the CEO of several companies and has worked all over the world. Before entering the corporate world, he was a fighter pilot in the Israeli air force and found himself in many situations that were uncomfortable, to say the least. Each year he likes to start something new. When I talked to him, he told me how he had taken up rock guitar and ice skating. He talked about how the ability to try something new and succeed has given him the confidence to keep trying new experiences. And that keeps him learning and growing. And each time he does this and succeeds, it builds his confidence. It is that confidence that allows you to pursue bigger activities.

His confidence, he told me, comes from both the head—having data to show you are succeeding—and the heart—the belief you can do more.

In 2017, my wife, two boys, and I traveled around the world, spending one year visiting twenty-nine countries. My oldest son, eleven at the time, was thrilled and willing to go anywhere and try any food. My youngest son, nine at the time, did not want to go on the trip and only wanted to eat pizza for the first few months. He did not like change or trying new foods or adventures. After a year of something new every day, he is a different kid. You can get comfortable being uncomfortable. But it is an uncomfortable process.

Chris Henry knows about taking risks. He is an interesting character, as he has cycled across the United States, down the west coast of the US, and walked the 500-mile Camino de Santiago in Spain. When I sat down with Chris, he was planning a 1,000-mile hike from Switzerland to Spain and a 2,650-mile bike ride from Canada to Key West. But if you saw him, you would not think he is a cyclist, as he does not have the thin body type like so many in that sport. Before these adventures, he was the vice president of sales for an international semiconductor manufacturer in Silicon Valley.

After Chris took over a new group, he realized one of the best opportunities was to build a subassembly with his device for a new customer: Apple. This would save Apple a year of software development. At the time, Apple was not the dominant player it would become, and Chris's CEO was hesitant to go down that path with Apple on a custom solution. Chris, believing that if you do not take risks, you do not get bigger, continued to explore the opportunity further until he had a more compelling argument for his boss. In their next meeting, the CEO relented and said, "Just don't take me someplace I can't get out of, and don't disrupt the company so much with your project." This gave Chris the necessary approval to move forward and eventually go from nothing at Apple to

$6 million in revenue after the first year and $35 million a couple years later. "If you do not take risks, you do not get bigger," he repeated to me.

Several years ago, I was consulting for a Fortune 100 manufacturing company with a very low risk tolerance. At the time, I was working with the finance executives for this Japanese-based company, who had an even lower risk tolerance. As the company's competitors were making more aggressive moves and gaining market share, I asked this group in what areas they could take more risks. The more senior member of the finance team turned to his colleague and said, "I am comfortable with us taking more risk as long as you take time to evaluate all the variables and weigh out the pros and cons to make sure we won't lose too much." Perplexed and realizing that as a consultant you must, at times, tell people things they do not want to hear, I said, "That is not taking risk." That company was recently surpassed in market share by its more risk-tolerant competitor.

> "If you do not take risks, you do not get bigger."
>
> **Chris Henry,** sales vice president, Xilinx

HANG WITH PEOPLE WHO GO A STEP FARTHER

Chris Fellows is the founder of the North American Ski Training Center (NASTC) and an author, adventurer, and international tour guide. He lives in Truckee, California, at the base of some of the greatest ski resorts in the country. His friends are skiers, backcountry guides, and rock climbers. Since he loves all those activities and has turned his passion into his career, he surrounds himself with others who have that same passion. By being in that "community" of like-minded adventure enthusiasts, he is motivated and inspired to do more since so many of his friends are doing amazing things.

I have a similar group of friends. For the past fifteen years, every

Sunday morning, we meet at a trailhead to either mountain bike or run in the foothills near our houses. Most have completed some ultra-endurance event, whether an Ironman, a one-hundred-mile bicycle ride, or a fifty-, one-hundred-, or two-hundred-mile run. At one point, four of us were training for the same fifty-mile run. Even though very few people have completed a fifty-miler, it is normal for this group. Intellectually, I realize it is not common. But when you surround yourself with people who do things that are not ordinary, you start to believe those things are normal. I never truly felt running two hundred miles through several nights in remote wilderness was crazy because I surround myself with people who, while they do not recognize it as normal, also do not see it as abnormal. The other advantage, as Chris told me, is that this same community can be your cheerleaders when you need a pick-me-up. And you can do the same for them.

IF SOMEONE ASKS, SAY YES

When I sat down to talk with Dr. David Haglund, superintendent of the fifteen-thousand-student Pleasanton Unified School District, I was surprised when he said he never thought he would live past thirty years old. He is calm, cerebral, and levelheaded. But he was not always that way. As a seventeen-year-old self-described smart-ass, he got involved with a lot of bad kids and left school before graduating. He never imagined himself going for the gold. His trajectory to overseeing one of the top-rated districts in the nation and top 1 percent in California came because people kept asking him to take on something bigger, and he kept doing it. Early in his life, he took the mindset that he would say yes to good opportunities and invest 100 percent into those where a spark was ignited. If the spark did not ignite, he would pass on to the next idea.

Earlier in his career and having just earned his administrative credential, Dr. Haglund was approached by his superintendent to build a virtual school. This was a new idea, but their visions were not aligned. She wanted to have a virtual school, while he wanted to transform the way teachers taught and the way students learned. As the two continued the discussion and visions came together, he agreed to take on the project. The fact that he "knew nothing for more than half the job was not a barrier because" as he says, "I am a learner and could ask enough questions to learn." The project was a success, and he opened the new school as principal. That "virtual school" concept came in handy when, during March of 2020, all fifteen thousand students moved home to learn virtually.

Ironically, about one year after we spoke, he approached me about heading up a $323 million school bond campaign—something I had no experience doing. I thought about our earlier conversation, and even though I had no experience, I could learn. He too had never been involved in a school bond campaign before, so we would go through it together. We both learned a lot and ran a strong campaign. But we lost by 624 votes. I never regretted saying yes and am proud of the work we did. Could I have done better? Yes. Could a more experienced campaign manager have won? Possibly. However, 65 percent of school bonds failed that year, while in a typical year 85 percent pass. Sometimes you take on projects and succeed. Sometimes you do not. Don't be afraid to take on something you know nothing about as long as it aligns with your values.

ACTIVITIES

QUESTIONS TO ASK YOURSELF

›   What have you not done because you were afraid to fail?
›   What could you do this year that would make you nervous?
›   How can you build up confidence to achieve one of the items from your bucket list?
›   How much do you want this goal? (0 – Not at all. 5 – I'm indifferent. 10 – I will regret it if I don't do it.)
›   What are you most afraid of?
›   How badly do you want this goal?

EXERCISES

›   Choose one item from your bucket list that makes you a little nervous to start.
›   Write down what makes you nervous about starting one of your bucket-list goals.
›   Write down all your fears of moving forward with this goal.

Chapter 3

HONE YOUR DREAM BIGGER STRATEGY

> "We overestimate what we can do in a year and underestimate what we can do in ten years."
> **Bill Gates,** founder, Microsoft

CHRIS HENRY, the former VP of sales who led the project with Apple as a client, knows that if you "dream small, you win small," so instead of trying to grow from $10 million to $10.5 million, aim for $20 million. You just might reach $13 or $14 million. Some would say you failed because you did not reach your goal. Chris looks at it differently: "It is better to fail at $13 million than succeed at $10.5 million."

To think big, you need to commit to a time and place to DREAM.

FIND A TIME AND SPACE

Nikki Barua, author of *Beyond Barriers*, overcame extraordinary life challenges and writes about how it is possible to break barriers when you feel trapped by fear or uncertainty. As I talked to her, she explained how important it is to be curious about what your possibilities are. She regularly spends time just thinking. Nikki has a thinking chair where she can comfortably sit down and ponder a specific topic. This involves choosing a topic or question to think about for an hour. "I do it about twice a week, and when I don't make the time, I don't feel good."

While Nikki has her thinking chair, others find they can clear their mind by meditating or staring into space or going for a long run. The key is to put yourself in an environment that will free you of the day-to-day distractions and just let your mind wander.

When do you get your best ideas or have your most creative thoughts? For me, they occur when my mind can run wild and when it is not focusing on the mundane. There is a reason so many leadership retreats are conducted offsite and away from the walls of the organization. Granted, it is an excuse to stay at a fancy hotel, visit a beautiful city, and participate in an unusual activity—often referred to as "team building." But it does get you into a different frame of mind, which stimulates your brain in a different way.

For five years, I have been facilitating an annual leadership retreat for one of my clients. Two of those years, we did it close to the office and people could go home at night, and three years, we did it far away. Not surprisingly, in those years when we were far away from the office and people could not go home each night, we had the highest level of engagement and the best ideas. Not only were they physically removed from distractions—they were also mentally removed and could focus on the objectives of the retreat more effectively.

Moving from the mundane to the unique changes how you think. Some of my best ideas have come when I was out in the wilderness on a long run or cruising down a country road on my bicycle. When I get those ideas, I will say, "Hey, Siri…" and have her write my idea down for future reference. Be careful about dreaming too much on those country roads, as I have found myself in a ditch after veering off the pavement. My lawyer has advised me to say, "Daydreaming while cycling can be dangerous." You have been warned.

Bill Johnston, CEO of Recovery Brands, started up a sustainable textile company where all his clothing is made from recycled material. When he came out of college in 2008, he had to join the workforce during the worst economic time since the Great Depression. As an avid backpacker, he loved the outdoors and started working for a company taking high school kids backpacking, with the final part of the trip being a strenuous mountain climb up Mt. Rainier. During the four years at that company, he fell deeper in love with the outdoors and realized he needed to do something to protect our planet. He told me that when he was out for a bike ride with a friend and veteran textile manufacturer, the idea of sustainable textiles was formed. To this day, Bill gets out on regular mountain bike rides to clear his mind and focus on the next big thing. He also finds that if he can backpack, it allows him to be away from his phone and other technology so he can shift his brain to bigger ideas.

Ask yourself: Do your most creative ideas come while you are sitting in a staff meeting or lathering up in the shower? At your desk on a conference call or while out on a run? On an airplane heading to that training session or while on the beach on vacation? I would venture to say, and many of my experts did too, that it is critical to take an extended break from the office and spend time thinking. It is why some progressive companies offer sabbaticals.

As I was talking to my former CEO, I asked him why he decided to put in a sabbatical program. After five years of service, every employee could get eight weeks of paid time off and do whatever they wanted. It was an easy answer, as he felt it was good for the company and good for the individual. For the company, there were two aspects. First, the employee came back more refreshed than from the standard two-week vacation that many of us never take. Second, it ensured the manager was training his or her replacement, as the time had to be taken all at once. The organization should never be reliant on one person. We often think, "We could never survive if that person left the company." But when the person resigned, the company survived. Or, people think, "I'm so busy I can't afford to take a vacation." More than likely, you are feeding an over-fed ego, and you can leave. Few of us are that important. Sorry.

As this CEO was getting ready to leave for his sabbatical, he told his assistant, "Only call me if the building is burning down. And even then, I probably cannot do anything about it." I have also heard this referred to as the "CNN Rule," meaning if the issue is not big enough to be a story on CNN, it likely is not big enough for me to be called. Deal with it. The CEO used his sabbatical to test out his replacement, who eventually took over the helm. But more importantly, he used it to think of how he needed to prepare the company for its next phase.

And while you are out on your bike, sitting on the beach, taking that sabbatical, or just daydreaming somewhere, have a way to store those aspirations.

CREATE A DREAM NOTEBOOK

A dream written down with a date becomes a goal. How often do you think of some great idea or fun adventure or a new concept and then forget it shortly thereafter? What methods do you have to track those ideas so you can easily refer to them later?

My wife and I love to travel and have been all over the world together to sixty countries. But we still have an extensive list of places we want to visit and adventures we want to experience. As we get ideas that make us both get excited, we write them down. Then every year when we develop our upcoming year's goals, budget, and plans, we look over the list. The kids are too young for some of the adventures, so we put a year next to that adventure when they will be old enough. So we have already started planning (or at least talking about) trips that are five years out. This is all made much easier, as we have a repository to store our ideas.

As I interviewed Matt Glerum and Candra Canning, an endurance athletic couple, they talked about their "Big Life Binder." Candra has climbed one of the Seven Summits, Denali, which at 20,310 feet is the highest mountain in North America, and Matt, a former CEO and competitive paddler, completed the 444-mile Yukon River Quest. Both know how to think big and are constantly dreaming even bigger. As I interviewed Candra, she said,

> Matt and I have the "Big Life Binder" and stick ideas or pictures in it when something sparks our interest. We brainstorm about adventures when we have time together, with our favorite being while on an airplane or a long car ride. We often take our Big Life Binder along to choose from the ideas we have stored there. We even have a white barf bag from an airplane trip with a few yearly goals scribbled on it.
>
> Matt and I prioritize this big dreaming time because from the very beginning of our marriage we agreed that the purpose of our marriage was to support each other to stretch further and accomplish bigger dreams together than we could on our own.

Liz Steblay is the founder and president of both PrōKo Agency, a successful human resource consulting firm, and Professional Independent Consultants of America (PICA), aimed at helping independent consultants thrive. In fact, she was one of the first people I talked to as I was getting ready to start my own consulting practice. Apparently, I wasn't the only one, as she realized a need after so many people kept asking her the same questions. In an effort to keep her business growing and moving forward, she takes herself out to lunch twice per year. Armed with a pen and a notebook, she writes down her dreams and wishes. She focuses on how she envisions the business or herself. And then she adds them to her notebook.

Technology has made note taking and tracking quite easy, and the available tools have a wide range in functionality. Some are nothing more than an electronic notecard such as the Notes app on the iPhone, while others are more robust programs like Microsoft OneNote or Evernote. I am an avid OneNote user, as it allows me to store ideas, include links to documents, websites, and files, and search for information.

The key is to occasionally refer to your Big Life Binder or notebook or OneNote for inspiration. Just because it is written down does not mean the idea has to be executed. As time goes by, priorities change, but it is good to have something that captures your list of ideas and ignites the next big adventure.

ACTIVITIES

QUESTIONS TO ASK YOURSELF

> What time of day are you most creative?
> When was the last time you deliberately thought about your future goals in a meaningful way? And how did it look?
> Where do you get your best ideas?
> Is there a physical location you can go and dream?
> When a big idea presents itself, what do you do with it?
> What does or will your dream notebook look like—where you store all your ideas?
> When was the last time you looked over your list of big ideas? Assuming you have one.

EXERCISES

> Develop a place to store all your ideas.
> Identify how often you will look at this list of ideas.

PILLAR II – PLAN

> "Failing to plan is planning to fail."
> **Benjamin Franklin,** inventor

PLAN

to make those goals a reality and move the vision to action. Once you can Envision what the future looks like, you can start charting a course to get there. This involves understanding the necessary tasks you need to complete as well as evaluating the potential roadblocks that could hamper your success.

SYNONYMS

PREPARE

STRATEGIZE

ACTION

DESIGN

FRAMEWORK

STRATEGIC PLANNING

DEFINE

DREAMING IS EASY. Doing is hard. I often let a big idea ruminate in my head for a while. The longer it stays with me, the more interested I am. The sign I am serious is when I tell someone. My wife often jokes that when I say, "I am thinking of..." she translates that to, "I have decided to...." So when I told her I was thinking of signing up to run the Tahoe 200, she knew it was more than a thought.

I had just completed a one-hundred-mile run, so I was in decent physical shape and figured I could build on the momentum. The difference between running one hundred miles and two hundred miles, while physically more demanding, is far more mentally taxing. Even though it is twice the distance, I expected to be on the trail for three to four times longer. That meant instead of running through one night, I would run through three, maybe four nights. I would also be in remote areas where a serious accident or an injury could require a helicopter evacuation, so the risk was higher. Developing a plan and assessing the obstacles and risks to get to the starting line was critical.

"EVERYBODY HAS A PLAN UNTIL THEY ARE PUNCHED IN THE FACE"

Mike Tyson uttered this elegant quote, and I can think of no better admonition for the importance of having a plan. And a Plan B. If you get into a boxing ring, you better plan to be punched in the face. When it happens, what will you do? If you plan to run a marathon, you better plan to have tired legs and blisters. And if you start up a company, you better plan to be low on cash at some point. Do you have ideas to reduce the chances of these happening and a strategy for when they do?

How detailed does the plan have to be? That is a question I hear a lot, and it varies greatly. Some spend so much time planning that they never get the project started. Then there are those who believe the entire plan can be written on a napkin. As someone who spent many years teaching project management classes, I would like to say there is a right answer. But what I have learned throughout my career and during my discussions with entrepreneurs, executives, and endurance athletes is that success comes in all shapes and sizes. My shorthand takeaway is this: not enough time spent figuring how to get to your destination will result in spinning your wheels in potentially the wrong directions, while too much time planning will result in never moving forward. You may have been looking for a clear-cut answer about the level of detail you need, but it's not that easy. The balance for me is different than the balance for you, which is different than the balance for your boss or your team.

There is good research that says upfront planning does correlate to increased success. One of the most comprehensive studies I read was conducted by KPMG Peat Marwick (now KPMG), which looked at large computer system projects over a ten-year period in the late 1980s and early 1990s. They found that "Most of the successful projects devoted between 6 and 15 percent of the total project hours to planning, project management, and control."[20] While project management and control occur after planning, planning still contributed significantly to the success. The other, more highly correlated finding was that "Objectives, scope, deadlines, expectations, budgets were reconciled up-front."[21] In other words, the clearer you are on your goals, the greater your chance of success.

While that study was conducted over thirty years ago, the findings are consistent with similar research today. The Project Management Institute, one of the leading authorities on the subject, wrote, "Inadequate planning is one of the major reasons why projects spin out of control."[22]

The challenge is finding the balance between not enough and too much planning.

BEHAVIORS (PLAN)

In order to help find that sweet spot, the Plan pillar is broken into these three behaviors:

1 **Get started:** I visualize what a successful end result looks like and can start moving forward without developing a complete plan.

2 **Develop the plan:** I develop a more thorough project plan and can prioritize those activities to accomplish my long-term goals.

3 **Assess your obstacles and risks:** I predict and evaluate potential roadblocks and then develop strategies to mitigate the impact.

Chapter 4

GET STARTED

> "Dead last finish is greater than did not finish, which is better than did not start."
> **Anonymous**

GETTING TO THE STARTING LINE of any endurance event is a lot harder than getting to the finish line. Think of training for a marathon. The average person spends four to five hours during the race, while they will spend four to five months training. They will really start to feel the pain on race day in the last third, so one only has to deal with being uncomfortable—well, actually miserable—for one to two hours. Except for a few months of rest with normal exercise, I was training extensively for almost two years before running two hundred miles. This consisted of about one year preparing for my first one-hundred-miler followed by about nine months preparing for the two-hundred-miler, with some weeks consisting of over thirty hours of training. So if you can get to the starting line, you can more than likely get to the finish line. But it takes a lot of work.

There is a tendency to get the plan in place, get all your ducks in a row, and have the vision completely set before beginning anything great. Ideally, that would be wonderful. In reality, you often need a little forward progress to start. If you want to run a marathon, do not wait to determine what race you will enter or to have your training plan set, just go out and buy a pair of shoes. If you want to start your own business, buy a domain registration. Both are small investments, and both move you forward. I wrote a draft business plan for my consulting practice sixteen years before I took on my first client. When I wrote the plan, I expected it would be about twenty years before I started up my business.

Putting a full-blown plan in place takes time and can be a daunting task, so do something less intimidating. Do something to get the ball rolling. And then, do something else. And then…The first step makes the second step possible, which makes the third step probable. Or as the famous Christmas song from *Santa Claus Is Comin' to Town* goes, "Put one foot in front of the other…and soon you'll be walking 'cross the floor." I am sorry if that earworm is now crawling around your head. Or if you don't recall that movie, think of a Rube Goldberg machine where one reaction starts the ball rolling, causing many more activities.

What other things can you do to start developing your plan to show commitment and continue forward progression? That first thing may be telling someone.

SAY THE BIG IDEAS OUT LOUD

While sitting down with Bill Wheeler, CEO and founder of Black Tie Transportation, I learned how he grew his company to 150 employees. He moves forty thousand people over a quarter-million miles per month. Bill appears to be constantly moving and coming up with ideas and has the energy of someone thirty years his junior. This showed as his office is surrounded by motorcycle racing paraphernalia, indicating his love of speed and adventure.

Bill shared with me how when he has an idea, he tells someone. And since he has just vocalized what he "plans to do," he then feels compelled to get it done. His motto is, "Don't commit to what you're not committed to." It was one of his greatest strengths yet biggest curses until he figured out how to deal with it.

While he was working with an executive coach and explaining how stressed he was because he was constantly having to implement these ideas, the coach asked, "Why do you feel compelled to complete every idea?" Bill's response was, "I just told someone about the idea." To which his coach not so calmly yelled, "Stop telling people." This story was an example to me of Bill's character. He's a man of his word, but he may have been taking it a bit too far. I have worked with many executives who are tremendously strong in certain areas. Those strengths, however, may become detrimental in the extreme. For Bill, and many of those executives, it is about finding the sweet spot. Bill didn't truly have to stop telling people his ideas, but he did start to figure out this balance and understand when he was making a promise to himself (or others) versus when he was merely brainstorming.

It is one thing to dream about an idea only in your head but vastly different when you tell someone. Your commitment goes up because now other people will know if you succeed. Or fail. Soon they will ask you, "How are you doing with your goal?" That added pressure is helpful. In writing this book, I often had people ask me, "How is the book coming along?" And when I knew I would see them again, I did not want to come up with the same answer. So I needed to make sure I was progressing. Granted, it adds stress, but that stress gets results. To take this one step forward, after you tell a trusted advisor, ask them to be your accountability partner.

THE INDISPUTABLE VALUE OF AN ACCOUNTABILITY PARTNER

This person will ask you how things are going and hold you accountable for forward progress. It can be as informal as a spouse asking you at dinner how things are going to a more formal coach who guides you through a plan and holds you to your commitments. In some cases, it works well if both people are working toward the same, or a similar, goal. Think of two people who want to lose weight and get in shape. In many cases, the hardest part is moving from the bed to the driveway. Knowing someone else is waiting for you is often that needed pressure to "motivate" you forward. You don't want to disappoint the other person, nor do you want to be the reason they don't get in shape.

Randy Haykin was a successful tech executive and venture capitalist. Since those tremendous achievements, he has started up a wine brand, taught business courses at UC Berkeley Haas School of Business and University of Cambridge School of Business, and coached over one hundred business leaders. He also founded the Gratitude Network, which guides social-impact nonprofit leaders using a Silicon Valley venture approach to expand their business. He recognizes his fortunate lifestyle and clearly has a lot to be grateful for.

> "Part of getting things done is being held accountable. The key thing is to have an accountability partner, and in this case, I created a whole bunch of partners."
>
> **Randy Haykin,** tech executive and venture capitalist

During one of his milestone birthday years, he wanted to celebrate "365 Days of Gratitude." His plan was every day to share one thing he was grateful for to his network. During his celebration, Randy realized he might want to harness the gratitude of others in his extensive network, and thus was born the Gratitude Network. He told a few people about his plan who he knew would hold him to his word. As he explained to me, "Part of getting things done is being held accountable. The key thing is to have an accountability partner, and in this case, I created a whole bunch of partners. I couldn't help but create the Gratitude Network because everyone was holding me accountable!" He also knew people were enjoying his daily moments of gratitude and didn't want to let them down.

Just because we have told someone doesn't mean we have to have everything figured out. That will come.

"DON'T GET IT RIGHT; GET IT WRITTEN"

With any solid goal, you eventually should write your idea down in unambiguous language. The popular SMART acronym says that all goals should be Specific, Measurable, Attainable, Relevant, and Timebound. However, sometimes to get started, you need to write it down in ambiguous language and massage it until it becomes clearer. My college English professor once said, "Don't get it right; get it written." Not a phrase you would expect from someone teaching you to master the written word. He was helping students get started on a writing project. Too often, he said, when beginning to write an essay, or a book, or a research report, we focus on getting everything perfect. Instead, we should spend the early part of writing on getting our ideas on paper. Then, go back and correct it so it is written in a more polished format. All great pieces of art start off as a sketch on the back of a napkin, a poorly written first draft, an arcane piece of clay, or an idea for a business. And then when it forms and becomes clearer, turn that ambiguous language into something more definitive to make it SMART.

Specifically define what shall be accomplished to limit confusion.

Measurable so you can track toward completion.

Attainable so it is realistic, yet also challenging.

Relevant to your higher-level work or personal goals and your values.

Timebound so you know when the goal is accomplished.

Writing down your idea, like telling someone, helps cement your accountability.

THE FIRST STEP IS SIGNING UP

Given enough time and money, we can accomplish almost anything. When someone thinks of a big idea and then instantly says, "I can't," what that person is likely saying is that they could not accomplish that goal now with their current resources. I see this all the time with the executives I coach. Many times, I have heard one of the executives talk about how their CEO wants to completely revamp a part of the business, and the executive is concerned that it cannot be done. What they are thinking is that it cannot be done NOW. But with time and resources, it most likely can be.

When Julie Cullivan, CIO of FireEye, stepped into a role she had never done, the CEO, whom she had worked for in the past, knew her capabilities. He quickly asked her to take on a project and finish it within nine months. The team was skeptical that it could be accomplished in that limited amount of time and was hesitant to start. Julie looked at it differently. She felt that if we start moving forward but do not get everything done in nine months, at least we will not be where we are today. We will have accomplished something, and it will be partially done. The question was would the team have accomplished enough to satisfy the CEO in those nine months? The project eventually took eighteen months, but they did get enough done in the first nine months to proceed further.

Ask yourself:

> ›   What are the minimally acceptable expectations?
> ›   What are the optimal expectations?
> ›   What can be done now?
> ›   What can be done tomorrow?

And while work projects often have a time frame, many of our personal goals have more flexibility.

When my future wife and I were traveling on our seven-month adventure around the world, we met a family doing a similar trip. Later that night we looked at each other and agreed we should do the same when we had kids.

Fast-forward through an engagement on the Great Wall of China, marriage, a first child, and a second child. We then looked ahead and said we would go around the world when our boys were nine and eleven. Shortly after returning from this second trip around the world, someone asked us, "What do you have to do to get started?" It is an easy answer, I explained: "Set a date when you want to go."

At least set a range in which you plan to accomplish this goal. In 2008 when our second child was born, we did not know that we would be leaving on June 11, 2017, but could reasonably say that we were targeting to leave when school got out in June 2017. Set a date then drive your plan to that date. Some of you may be asking, how can you plan that far in advance? I say, how can you not? Granted, there could have been things that happened in those nine years, and a lot did happen, but nothing big enough to cause us to change course.

Ironman Steve Sherman told me the hardest part of an Ironman is signing up. Once you pay the exorbitant entrance fee, you are committed. Signing up does several things. First, it clearly outlines a date when you must be ready. Second, it financially ties you into the project or puts *some skin in the game.* By knowing when the race begins, you can back into your training plan. But if you do not have that start date, you can continually push the start of your training further down the road.

If you are serious about an idea, do something that gets you emotionally and financially invested. If it is a race, pay the registration fee. If you are looking to build a business, buy the website, develop a business plan, or design a prototype. Do something. Several venture capitalists I spoke with, when assessing if they want to invest in a company, ask the founder how much of their money they have put in. The more money one has contributed to the venture, the more they will be personally tied to the business's success. And the harder they will work to reach the goal. VCs like when you have your own money in the business because you are hungrier and more committed. And all the while, visualize what success looks like.

VISUALIZE THE FINISH LINE

A friend was working to pass a legal exam and had failed three times. In those three prior times, she only missed by a few points. She knew the material and had studied harder than her peers but was just not passing the exam. I asked her why she thought this was occurring, given that she knew the material so well. Her response was, "I'm nervous when I walk into the room." Understandable.

I suggested for a few weeks before the next exam that, as she was going to bed, she should imagine walking into the room with confidence.

I said, "Imagine the proctor handing you the exam and then you placing it on your desk with confidence. Imagine holding your head high, feeling healthy, feeling ready. And then imagine starting the test and thinking, 'This is easy.' Then keep imagining how easy the test is and as you finish, with ease, turn it in, and walk out of the room thinking, 'I nailed it.' And lastly, imagine a few weeks later going to the mailbox to retrieve a letter from the testing agency and opening it to read, 'Congratulations, you passed.' "

My goal was to shift her mind, so she was seeing what success looked like versus what failure looked like. She already knew what failure looked like, as she had seen it three other times. If you cannot see where you are going, it's hard to know when you've arrived. My job was to get her to see the future positively.

I have used this technique many times because if you know what success looks like, you are more apt to reach it. Professional athletes do the same. Michael Phelps, the most decorated Olympian of all time, holds twenty-eight medals—twenty-three are gold. Before a race, he uses visualization and relaxation techniques to help him prepare and get him into the zone.

The Blue Angels, before stepping into the cockpit of their F/A-18 Hornet and performing their highly aerobatic routines, sit in a conference room. With eyes shut, they talk through and visualize the entire routine. Failing a legal exam or touching the wall a hundredth of a second after the swimmer in the lane next to you sucks. Missing a maneuver at five hundred miles an hour is deadly.

The *Journal of Consulting Psychology* conducted a study on visualization for job seekers:

> One group of job seekers received traditional career counseling and interview coaching. Those in the second group were exposed to the same career counseling and interview training,

but these job seekers also learned to use visualization techniques related to these subjects.

Two months after the training, 21 percent of those in the group who did not use mental imagery found new jobs. But 66 percent of those who used this technique were employed within two months.[23]

The technique is simple. Several weeks beforehand, begin your visualization. In a quiet room—you can do this as you are going to sleep—imagine walking into your situation. Imagine that you feel good and are comfortable, confident, and ready. Define success and then imagine accomplishing what you have just defined. Since challenging times are inevitable, imagine those as well. But imagine how you easily made it through those times and still came out on top. The ability to see the future while still in the present just may be the difference between success and failure. I and many I spoke with have used this to start a company, climb a mountain, write a book, reach financial independence, pivot their business, and reach so many large peaks in their life—even pass a law exam.

I have routinely used this technique when I coached leaders getting ready to give big presentations. Most people get nervous when they speak to large groups. They are afraid they will fail, the audience will sit there stone faced, or nobody will laugh at their jokes. So for several weeks prior, I encourage speakers, as they go to bed, to imagine the audience is fully engaged, sitting up straight listening, taking notes, laughing, smiling, and then clapping loudly as they finish their last words.

Visualize what you want, not what you fear.

A few weeks after that friend took her legal exam, she walked to the mailbox, just as she imagined, and opened the letter from the testing agency. "Congratulations, you passed."

ACTIVITIES

QUESTIONS TO ASK YOURSELF

> What is the first step you will make?
> Whom will you tell?
> Who would be a good accountability partner?
> When will you start this goal?
> When do you want to finish?
> What have you written down to make this more real?
> What does "success" look like?
> What are all the benefits you will get when you are successful?

EXERCISES

> Write down on your calendar one activity you can start in the next seventy-two hours that moves you forward with one of your goals.
> Set an approximate date when you plan to achieve one of your goals.
> Tell someone what you are committing to.
> Ask someone to hold you accountable.
> Paint a picture in your head or write down how it will look and how you will feel when you complete your big idea.

Chapter 5

DEVELOP THE PLAN

"A goal without a plan is just a wish."
Antoine de Saint-Exupéry, poet

As an air force pilot, USAF Academy graduate, and Ironman, Diann Boyle said, *"Prior Planning Prevents Piss Poor Performance"*—or, as she called it, her "6 Ps." The amount of planning varied dramatically between the people I interviewed. Some did their planning on the back of a napkin and then jumped into the deep end. Some did a more thorough analysis, started in the baby pool, and worked their way into deeper waters. But all spent some time thinking about the future and how to get there.

MOVE ONE GRAIN OF SAND AT A TIME

A dream *written down with a date becomes a goal. A* goal *broken down into steps becomes a* plan. *A* plan *backed by action becomes* reality. Or another way to put it, write it down, break it down, then get down to business. Most big projects are daunting. You cannot see the end, the middle is murky, and the start is unclear. That is normal and part of the process. The more you can break your big goal into smaller chunks, the easier it is to more clearly see the different areas.

After Alicia Wallace visited Sierra Leone in western Africa for the first time and saw how big an issue poverty was on the continent, she was overwhelmed. But she knew she could solve big problems. I asked her how she thought she could solve that one, and her response caught me off guard. She said, "I learned to think like an ant." My immediate response was, "What?" until she explained. "When ants want to build a house, they move one grain of sand at a time." She came to this realization after buying an ant farm and watching how the wall of sand eventually turned into mazes and tunnels and then the home for the colony. This gave her the energy to start somewhere and not worry exactly where she was going. Of course, that initial ant farm did not start smoothly. When it arrived in the mail, most of the ants were dead. Being creative, she went into the backyard, found some ants, and introduced them to her colony. Sometimes you need to improvise.

Standing at the starting line of the Tahoe 200 was also daunting. While I knew exactly where the finish line was—since it was one very long 205-mile loop, I was standing at my final destination—I did not know when I would arrive or even IF I would arrive. I did not know how I would feel along the way. But I was relatively confident I would be tired and miserable at some points. So if I focused on running 205 miles, I would potentially mentally push myself too far. I broke it into smaller chunks. There are fifteen aid stations placed around the course, spread out anywhere from 7 miles to 26 miles apart. So instead of thinking, "I have 148 more miles to go," I would think, "I only have 6 more miles to the next aid station." And then I would think of all the good things I could experience when I arrived. My wife would be there. I could eat a warm meal.

I could put on a new pair of socks and shoes. And then as I left that aid station, I would think, "Only seventeen more miles until I can see my wife and eat some potato chips." There are times you want to see the finish line, but there are times you just need to focus on the next milestone.

A newly promoted president of a European company I spoke with was asked to take over a failing business. With only one year left on his contract and enough money to retire, he saw a big challenge. He told me, "The company was totally broken, and the team was not motivated, as 50 percent were fired the year before. Other people failed before me, so expectations were low." The board had considered closing down the business, which would cost $200 million, so this person was given one year to turn things around. Or as his boss said to him, "Take all the time you need, but do it quickly."

He promptly defined his goal to rebuild the company and move it to profitability within five years by focusing on two areas: 1) his team and 2) the company's suppliers. Being good at figuring out the details, he built a plan and, being a self-described control freak, focused on the milestones. Every time there was a success or increase in morale, he would revel in it. Focusing on the goal and its corresponding milestones worked as he grew sales from $325 million to $1.3 billion with 7 percent profitability. While this newly appointed president turned things around by breaking down his goal into key milestones, his intense focus on priorities was a major factor.

HOW WILL YOU PRIORITIZE YOUR SIXTY-TWO HOURS EACH WEEK?

When choosing large endeavors, we need to prioritize how we use our time and how we spend our money. Time is about where we focus our energy. Is it staying up late partying with friends, sitting on the couch reading a book, getting up early to go for a run, working late in the office, or taking every vacation day to be with your family? Everyone has different priorities, which are driven by their values. Remember when you looked at your values earlier in this book?

We all have the same number of hours in a day: 24. We all have the same number of days in a week: 7. We all have the same number of days in a year: 365. It is how we use that time that says what is most important to each of us. Granted, we don't all have the same number of years, but most of us will have 60 to 70 years. If you want to see your priorities, look at your calendar.

Money varies widely for everyone. I interviewed a range of people, from those who have millions of dollars and names that are on university buildings to those who have little in their savings account. Where we spend that money shows what we value. Look at your calendar to see where you prioritize your time, and check your budget to see where you prioritize your money. Actually, check the "actuals" or your credit card or with your CFO to get a more accurate picture. I have coached others in the past and asked to look at their calendar and the company's spending. So when someone says they value people, I can see if they really mean it.

Fundamentally, most of us spend our time in three broad categories: 1) working; 2) sleeping; and 3) living.

WORKING

This may involve an average forty-hour-per-week job and commuting to and from your office. But let's be honest: if you're reading this book, you're probably working more than forty hours. If you are a student, then "school" is your work, or if you are a stay-at-home parent, then laundry, shopping, cooking, cleaning, and taking kids to school is your work. And probably a million other things—my wife is a stay-at-home mom and clearly works harder than I do.

SLEEPING

This one should make sense, but are you doing enough of this? Sleep experts recommend eight hours per day. Are you paying attention to the experts?

LIVING

This involves eating, hanging out with your family, watching TV, reading, recreating, travel, and completing a variety of mundane tasks that just need to be done to keep the lights on.

Assuming a ten-hour workday (including commute) and eight hours of sleep, that means that we spend approximately a third of our time in each area. We likely have the least amount of flexibility in "Work" and then "Sleep." So according to the table below, we have, on average, sixty-two hours per week to "Live."

	WORK	SLEEP	LIVE	TOTAL
MONDAY	10	8	6	24
TUESDAY	10	8	6	24
WEDNESDAY	10	8	6	24
THURSDAY	10	8	6	24
FRIDAY	10	8	6	24
SATURDAY	-	8	16	24
SUNDAY	-	8	16	24
TOTAL (WEEK)	50	56	62	168
TOTAL (YEAR)	2,600	2,912	3,224	8,736
TOTAL (PERCENT)	30%	33%	37%	

I realize the numbers will vary significantly for each person, so take a few minutes and calculate your totals. It is much easier than you may imagine. What time do you go to work, and what time do you get home? That is the "Work" category. What time do you normally go to bed, and what time do you normally get out of bed? That is the "Sleep" category. Subtract those two numbers from twenty-four, and you figure out your "Live" category. Do that for each day of the week. Now that you know the numbers, you can start to reprioritize where you spend your time.

When training for the Tahoe 200, I knew that some weeks my training would take up to thirty hours. I needed to find that time from one of these three areas. I chose not to reduce my sleep, and, in fact, sometimes had to take an afternoon nap after a long training day. The body needs the rest to recuperate after intense workouts, so this was nonnegotiable for me. As an independent consultant, I then had the choice to reduce either my family or work time. I chose to reduce the number of clients I took on for the nine months leading up to the race, as I did not want to cut back on my family time. I realize that I was fortunate to make that decision where others do not have that option. However, with a fixed resource (hours), you must decide how you will allocate your energy.

There are times it is great to have a balance between work and life. But if you are going to excel in one area, you must give up something in another area. Very few company founders told me they had a work-life balance when they were starting something great. Understanding your balance goes directly back to knowing your values and purpose (Envision) and what you hope to achieve long term. Now that you understand where your time and money are being spent, reduce the unimportant tasks and reallocate your energy and dollars to those more important initiatives.

ACTIVITIES

QUESTIONS TO ASK YOURSELF

› What short-term goals have you set to accomplish your longer-term dreams?
› How have you made time to reach your goal?
› What are the most important elements to accomplishing this goal?
› What activities or tasks would need to be removed or reduced to make time for this new priority?

EXERCISES

› Break your goal down into manageable chucks by writing down the five to ten milestones that need to be accomplished.
› Calculate your Work / Sleep / Live hours and adjust to make time for this goal.

	WORK	SLEEP	LIVE	TOTAL
MONDAY				
TUESDAY				
WEDNESDAY				
THURSDAY				
FRIDAY				
SATURDAY				
SUNDAY				
TOTAL (WEEK)				
TOTAL (YEAR)				
TOTAL (PERCENT)				

Chapter 6

ASSESS OBSTACLES AND RISKS

> "I'm not a risk-taker; I'm a risk manager."
> **Ed Viesturs,** mountain climber

IT IS GOOD TO BE NERVOUS AT TIMES. If we live in a world when our heart is always thumping at a normal rate, our palms are never sweaty, and butterflies are not flying around in our belly, we probably are not living an overly exciting life. Some people like that lifestyle and likely won't read this book. But given that you are, I bet you realize some level of discomfort and risk in life is normal and healthy.

There are many obstacles that will get in our way so we must first figure out the ones that are most likely to have the greatest impact.

1. Physical (break a limb, fall, or get cut)
2. Emotional (fear or sadness)
3. Psychological (self-fulfilling prophecy and not allowing for a positive outcome or trauma)

4. Financial (loss of investments/revenue or unexpected expenses)
5. Business (loss of major customer, industry downturn)

Write down the ones that have the potential to cause you the most concern so you can figure out how to reduce your exposure. As you look over your list, truly assess whether you have a fear that is a psychological barrier causing you paralysis or a risk that has some statistical probability of the event happening. Both are real. Both can hold you back. It's important that you're honest with yourself so that you can take action accordingly.

WHAT DOES YOUR RISK CALCULATOR LOOK LIKE?

Most of the people I talked with, when asked, "What is your view on risk?" answered similarly. They said, "I take calculated risks." And while they all use a different "calculator," none of them jump into the water without first looking down. Some peek over the cliff to see what is down there, then leap. Some toss a rock to see how deep it is. Some walk down to the water's edge and slowly enter the river. But all make some level of assessment to understand what they are getting into.

If you have ever watched a kayaker purposefully go over a waterfall, you must think they have a death wish. What you often do not see is that for quite some time beforehand, they and their fellow paddlers are standing at the top of the falls assessing the situation. They are looking for obstacles like trees, branches, or rocks. They are watching for eddies, the flow of the current, and the strength of the wind. They are determining where to enter the top of the falls and where they come out at the bottom. And they are evaluating their exit strategy in case something does go wrong. They do not want to die; they want to live.

Every large-scale project I worked on had something go wrong. And every seasoned project manager I know would say the same. This is the time to think about what could potentially go wrong and plan to minimize it. And then also prepare for if it does happen. What is your plan?

In the documentary *Kim Swims*, Kim Chambers swam 26.2 miles over seventeen hours from the shark-infested waters of the Farallon Islands to the Golden Gate Bridge in the Pacific Ocean near San Francisco, California. Her training partner and Australian marathon swimmer, Simon Dominguez, also attempted the swim one week prior but in the reverse direction, ending in the shark-infested waters near the Farallon Islands. A few weeks before the swim he was asked if he had a death wish. Simon's response was:

> You are swimming in freezing cold water, with strong tides, out to an area that is full of great white sharks. That doesn't sound like a reasonable thing to do. And I said to this person, that is a fair question, but these swims are very much calculated risks. We plan the right time of year so there aren't as many sharks. We spend years and years of training in the cold water to make sure our body is used to the cold. We have a lot of experts who look at the tides and the currents and advise us. Yes, it is risky. Yes, it is dangerous. But it is a hell of a lot of fun as well.[24]

Most of us wouldn't find swimming with the sharks fun. It is more risk than we would want to endure, but we can at least understand the risks and how to reduce the critical ones.

Granted, we all have different levels. Entrepreneur Shane Kenny admits he has a high risk tolerance. After selling his high-tech company his brother, Aaron Kenny, and he started, they found themselves with a nice pot of change. Shane says there are two types of people who have made it. There are

> "Yes, it is risky. Yes, it is dangerous. But it is a hell of a lot of fun as well."
>
> **Simon Dominguez,**
> endurance swimmer

those people who had a big win and take the money and keep it safely protected so it will last the rest of their life. Then, there are those people like Elon Musk or Richard Branson who continue to risk everything.

While Elon is often associated with Tesla or SpaceX, those companies were funded because of the money he earned from selling PayPal for $1.5 billion to eBay. But the money for PayPal was earned from two earlier ventures, including the first company he started with his brother, then sold for $350 million to Compaq.

Richard Branson is equally risky and earned his initial wealth from a mail-order record business that he grew to be Virgin Records. From that, he continued to invest in a variety of businesses, including publishing, clothing, cola, airlines, and space. Some survived. Some died. And while he risked his wealth many times, he also risked his life setting hot-air balloon records and taking a trip to space. In his book, *Like a Virgin*, Branson wrote, "I suppose the secret to bouncing back is not only to be unafraid of failures but to use them as motivational and learning tools.... There's nothing wrong with making mistakes as long as you don't make the same ones over and over again."

After Shane explained that there are two types of people, I asked him which one he was. "While I have a high risk tolerance, there is a pool of money that isn't touchable," he said, then paused and jokingly added, "It doesn't mean I wouldn't touch it." Even then, I believed there was a hint of seriousness in that last comment.

Fast forward two years. I guess I wasn't too surprised when I talked to him after our initial discussion, and he told me how he and his wife sold all their possessions and most of their investments and bought a beach club on the Caribbean Sea. He then said, "We essentially took the 'risk it all again' approach." I'm not sure Shane and I have the same definition of "untouchable."

Where are you on that risk continuum?

TAKE THE SLEEP TEST

Ben is the vice president in product marketing at an enterprise software company. While that is his day job, he is also an Ironman and real estate investor in the San Francisco Bay Area. In an area of the country where it is hard to find much for under a million dollars, he has put a lot of money on the line at times. At one point, he was 90 percent leveraged, meaning that for every dollar of equity, he owed ninety cents. It is risky, and there were many nights he did not sleep so well. "For one stressful year I was only getting four to five hours of sleep because of the debt load, and we were in constant renovations on one of the properties. Every day there was a new expense," he told me. Before making these big investments, he broke down the problems into these three areas:

1. What if I lost my job?
2. What if a renter moved out?
3. What if the renovation costs increased?

"If I focused on the big fear—bankruptcy—it would cripple me, so I had to break it down." He then went on to say, "And from each one of these, I looked at ways to reduce the probability and the impact. I kept thinking through the worst-case scenarios and what I could do to reduce the chances of those occurring. The fact that I had a plan in place and focused on that plan helped me sleep a little better at night."

Financial advisors use a similar "sleep test" to assess your comfort level with investments. The S&P Index since its inception in 1926 has earned between 10 and 11 percent. In 1931 it was down 47 percent and in 2008 down 38 percent. In the early part of the coronavirus pandemic, it was down 34 percent. Conversely, it was up over 45 percent in 1933 and 1954.[25] And about one year after hitting its low from the pandemic, it was up almost 80 percent. While it is great to be invested in the years the money goes up significantly, if you cannot handle the steep downturns and find yourself up late at night not sleeping, you may be taking too much risk. It is important to understand your comfort level with risk. If you can't sleep, it might be just too much for you.

BE YOUR OWN RISK MANAGER

Risk is something that one can manage. In fact, here is an excerpt from a job description for a risk manager. Yes, that is a real job.

> As a risk manager, you are in charge of determining financial, safety and security risks for a company or organization, and you find ways to reduce those risks through planning and problem-solving. Risk managers are in charge of research activities such as risk assessment for current company affairs or risk evaluation, which evaluates the company's handling of risks in the past.

Your role during this phase is as a risk manager: to assess the probability and impact of risks, and then determine a mitigation plan. In essence, you are trying to identify if you need a safety net under you and how big and strong that net should be.

I'm guessing the swimmers referenced earlier weren't too excited to be so close to sharks and there was a little bit of fear, but they assessed the probability of getting attacked. At the beginning, they felt the risk was low enough. Then Simon approached the end of his twenty-six-mile swim. Exhausted and moving around like a tired seal, he was being circled by a great white. He and his team assessed the situation and realized the probability of danger had now grown and was too high. He got in the boat and didn't finish his epic goal. To reduce the chance of this happening again, Kim reversed her course, so she started at the Farallons, where the sharks were more prevalent, but she was not looking like a tired seal, as she was fresh. No shade to Simon and his team. Both

Kim and Simon are inspiring athletes. The point is simply that risks and obstacles are also a game-time decision and really a series of moment-to-moment decisions. When conditions change, will you be prepared and willing to change course? That's what managing risk is about.

Below are some questions to ask yourself so you can manage those moments.

What is the worst-case scenario?

Include everything that could possibly go wrong. Humans are wired to think about the worst thing that could happen.

What is the realistic bad-case scenario?

Now that you have written down your worst-case scenario, which likely involves death, complete loss of all your money, company insolvency, or some other catastrophic event, what is a more realistic bad-case scenario? Rarely does the worst-case scenario happen, whereas a realistic bad-case scenario is more frequent. My worst-case scenario for Tahoe was getting attacked by a bear and being left for dead in the remote wilderness. My realistic bad-case scenario was breaking my ankle and needing to be evacuated. So all those "bears" I saw in the beginning made me wonder if I would be eaten alive. Spoiler Alert: I wasn't.

What is the impact?

If one of these scenarios were to occur, evaluate whether it is a high, medium, or low impact to your life or those around you, the organization, or the situation.

What is the chance this will occur?

Evaluate if there is a high, medium, or low chance of occurrence and the impact.

If the chance AND impact are low, do not worry about it and move on to the next problem. And there is always a "next problem." If the chance AND impact are high, you need a risk mitigation plan. If chance of the bad situation occurring is high and the impact is low OR the impact is high and the chance is low, you should explore further and look at the next two questions as part of your risk mitigation plan.

	LOW	HIGH
HIGH	YOUR CALL	NEED PLAN
LOW	DON'T WORRY	YOUR CALL

(vertical axis: IMPACT — HIGH to LOW; horizontal axis: CHANCE OF EVENT HAPPENING — LOW to HIGH)

What is your plan to prevent or reduce the risk of its impact? Or what can you do to minimize the impact it will have if the negative event does occur?

How will you respond if the situation were to happen? What WILL you do if your worst-case or bad-case scenario occurs?

It is good to have this in place before things turn bad because at that time, you may not be thinking as rationally as you would like.

GET READY FOR THAT "OH SHIT" MOMENT

Problems will occur; that is almost guaranteed. Your job is to try to keep those from happening but also to be prepared for when they do happen. Have a game plan in place for when they do. If you have ever remodeled part of a house, you likely experienced the contractor saying, "We just found something we didn't plan for."

My dad was a contractor and built custom homes. My brother followed in his footsteps. I, on the other hand, lack most skills related to that profession but heard many stories and have overseen a few remodels in my own homes. I know that when you start a remodel, you cannot see all the problems behind every wall, above every ceiling, or under every subfloor. Inevitably there will be dry rot, a pipe that has corroded, faulty electrical wiring, or some other unexpected "joy." If you have never experienced this, turn on any remodel program on HGTV, and you will see what I am talking about. Halfway through the show, the host approaches the homeowner and says, "I've got some bad news…." In TV production land, they call that a "narrative arc." On your land, in your house, during your remodel, it's called an "Oh shit" moment.

Rarely have I seen a construction project, or any other type of project, go as planned. If you have a budget that does not take into account any unforeseen costs, you will more than likely go over that amount. And if you cannot spend more, you will be stressed. As the wife of a contractor, my mom would always tell friends, "Double the budget and double the time." Remember, shit will happen. It always does. So expect it and plan for it.

DO YOU HAVE A PLAN Z?

If Plan A does not work, keep in mind you have twenty-five more letters in the alphabet. It is good to have a backup plan in case things go awry.

Albert Dyrness is the founder and managing director of a 130-person engineering consulting business. He is able to take more risks, as he has a backup plan in place. Engineers are not known, whether accurately or not, for being risk-takers, although I have worked with many who are. Engineers build things to not fail. They test, retest, and test again. And then after all the testing, they build in redundancy systems for the rare instance if something does fail. This is why flying is so safe, because if one engine goes out on the Boeing 747 you are flying across the Atlantic Ocean, three others will safely take you to your destination.

Albert came from a background where his family did not go to college, and many were in construction. So construction was always his backup plan, but he wanted to go to college and be an architect. He thought, if architecture did not work, he could be a draftsman, and if that did not work, he could be in construction. He eventually pursued engineering but always had his Plans B, C, and D ready. He said, "I am conservative, which is likely why I only got to a 130-person business. I like to have one toe in crazy, and the rest of the foot is safe." But then the next person I talked to surprised me about her contingency plan.

Heather Brien is a partner at a private equity firm, president of the board of directors for the nonprofit CASA San Mateo, and an ultra-distance endurance athlete. She explained how she likes to build contingencies into her plan. Many people shared theirs, but she took it to a new level. While pregnant, Heather signed up for an Ironman (remember, that is a 2.4-mile swim, 112-mile bike ride, and 26.2-mile run) that was scheduled only six months after she gave birth to her son. She wasn't sure if that would be enough time to recover, so she had a backup race—her contingency plan—only nine weeks after her target race. She wanted to make sure if she couldn't complete the first one, she felt confident she'd be ready for the next one.

> "I like to have one toe in crazy, and the rest of the foot is safe."
>
> **Albert Dyrness,** founder and managing director of an engineering consulting firm

When my wife, our two boys, and I traveled around the world for a year, there was a possibility that everything we owned could be stolen. Passports, computers, clothes—everything. We talked about how to minimize the chances of this happening, but we also talked about what we would do if it did happen. Losing our passport in the middle of Africa would have a significant impact and was something we needed to plan for. Fortunately, it never happened, but I sure did sleep better knowing we had a plan in case it did. Contingency plans should help you sleep better at night and, if problems do occur, help you manage the difficulties.

ACTIVITIES

QUESTIONS TO ASK YOURSELF

> What obstacles (physical, mental, financial, time, etc.) are in your path toward success?
> How can you reduce those obstacles?
> What criteria will you use to stop or pivot?
> How many things would have to go wrong before a catastrophe?

EXERCISES

> Identify the two to three most realistic obstacles you will face.
> Evaluate the chance each obstacle will occur and the impact if they do occur.
> Define the worst thing that could happen if you fail.
> Define the most realistic worst-case scenario that could happen.

PILLAR III — ITERATE

> "The process of doing something, again and again, usually to improve it. It is about experimenting, practicing, and repeating to get better."
> **Cambridge Dictionary**

ITERATE

your plan to work out the kinks and practice for the difficult times. It is about executing smaller components of your overall goal and finding the flaws. It is a chance to fix those flaws and improve the situation before going primetime. It is also about trying new things and seeing how they work. During this phase, you are working toward perfection, but that is not the goal.

SYNONYMS

TRAIN

PRACTICE

CONTINUOUS IMPROVEMENT

FAILURE ANALYSIS

CUSTOMER FEEDBACK

STRESS TESTING

EXPERIMENT

REPETITION

I LOVE PLANS BECAUSE they have always given me a road map for where I am going and how I will get there. And while a road map is good, I have never, ever, had a project go exactly as planned.

Iterate may not be a word you use every day, as you may use one of its synonyms. In sports this is called "training." In structural engineering, it is called "failure analysis." In science, it is called "experimenting." In some organizations, it is called "continuous improvement." Some industries call it "AB testing." In software development, it is called "testing." It's also called "iterating." Whatever term you use, it is about trying, failing, tweaking, and trying again until you get it more right and then moving on. It is the repetition of a task to get better and then be able to take on bigger aspects of the tasks.

When Elon Musk started SpaceX, he knew it would take several attempts to successfully launch a rocket into orbit. He didn't immediately shoot the first rocket into space, but he put it on the launch pad, then shot off the engines with the vehicle never leaving earth. He did that several times and then eventually practiced with the vehicle leaving the launch pad for a short distance. He learned from each test and adjusted for the next time. Then off to low earth orbit before going higher and eventually docking with the International Space Station.

Iterating is about starting small, learning, making adjustments, and trying again.

YOU CAN'T REACH SUCCESS OVERNIGHT

I live in the heart of Silicon Valley, where people think everyone is a millionaire and has started up a technology company. I have had friends who have been multimillionaires one year and then lost it all the next year. We see young millionaire (or billionaire) CEOs on the news all the time, but that is the exception, not the rule. So there is a misconception that you can easily make it overnight. Few do. Statistically, you probably won't.

Success rarely happens overnight and often involves a lot of hard work, failed attempts, retries, and more hard work. Most of us want to find the Get Rich Quick scheme—heck, I sure do—but there are more trusted methods. I typed "Get Rich Quick" into Google and found twenty-nine million results. It would be quicker for me to develop a good idea and work hard to implement that idea than to read through all these entries, most of which are unproven or ill-conceived at best, and more than likely immoral or illegal. Actor Adrien Brody said, "My dad told me, 'It takes fifteen years to be an overnight success,' and it took me seventeen and a half years." Overnight successes are few and far between. If it happens, great. That is not what this book is about. So if you are looking for overnight success, thanks for making it this far, but you might want to put it down and look for something else. I would venture to guess you'll generate better results faster if you keep reading than if you follow a Get Rich Quick promise.

THE EMOTIONAL JOURNEY OF CREATING ANYTHING GREAT

The journey to anything great is not easy. While we often only see the tremendous success like the CEO ringing the opening bell at the stock market after an IPO, a founder selling his company for $5 billion, a climber putting a flag on the top of a summit, or an employee receiving Top Salesperson at an annual company gathering, the path from idea to finish is filled with potholes, fights, doubt, fear, excitement, and failures.

This makes me think of the scene from *A League of Their Own* when Dottie, played by Geena Davis, is approached by her manager as he sees her ready to drive home and quit the team. Dottie says to the manager, played by Tom Hanks, "It just got too hard." He passionately responds, "It's supposed to be hard. If it wasn't hard, everyone would do it. The hard is what makes it great."

This is a common journey many of the entrepreneurs and endurance athletes shared with me. There are times you feel like you are on top of the world and times you feel the world is on top of you. There are days you question your sanity, competence, or ability to reach your goal, and then there are days when you feel as if nothing can stop you.

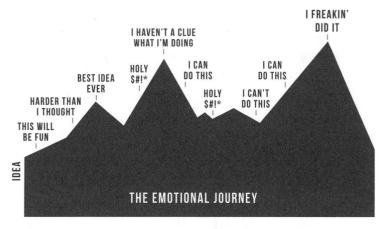

Everything starts with an idea. When you share that idea with others, they may tell you, "You're crazy." Some may exuberantly say, "That's cool; when do we start?" Don't be surprised if many just shrug their shoulders and say, "OK." What matters is what you think of the idea and your commitment to it. There will be times when what you are working toward is a lot of fun, but more often there will be days of sheer exhaustion, and the only thing that keeps you moving forward is your belief in the mission. Therefore, it is so important to be clear on why you started this ambitious project and understand both the emotional price in the middle AND the emotional payoff at the end.

Being clear on your WHY and your "emotional payoff" is critical, as this will get you through the challenging times. When you're talking about EPIC Performances, it is relatively easy to "Envision" an idea, "Plan" it out, and "Collaborate," but the heavy lifting is during "Iterate" and "Perform." Talk to any athlete, and they will tell you Iterate (i.e., training or practice) often represents the longest and most difficult part of the journey to the finish line.

Consider this. It takes four to five months of focused training to arrive at the starting line for a marathon and only four to five hours to get to the finish line. I have always figured that if I can make it to the starting line healthy and injury free, I can make it to the finish line. Just remember, *The hard is what makes it great.*

BEHAVIORS (ITERATE)

These three behaviors will help you successfully Iterate:

1 **Practice with intention:** I achieve success in shorter-term projects so I can work up to accomplish my bigger dreams while also building in routines to be more efficient with my time.

2 **Apply the data:** I define objective success criteria and evaluate my performance against those measures.

3 **Manage obstacles and risks:** I remove potential issues or roadblocks that could impact my focus and success.

Chapter 7

PRACTICE WITH INTENTION

> "Practice doesn't make perfect. Practice reduces the imperfection."
> **Toba Beta,** author

HAVING A PICTURE of what success looks like is a critical element in reaching any major endeavor. All along the way, there will be many obstacles. Your goal is to focus more on the path forward than the walls blocking your way.

FOCUS ON THE WHITE

The former CEO of enterprise software company Documentum, Jeff Miller, relayed this story to me about when he was heli-skiing in the remote wilderness. He and his pals were dropped off at the top of the mountain well above the tree line. As they clicked their boots into their skis and adjusted their goggles, they could see nothing but white snow ahead. It was a beautiful day with a long ski run in front of them. As they made their way down the mountain, they dropped into the tree line. Some of the more experienced skiers easily worked their way through the trees, but all Jeff could see were the trunks and branches blocking his way. The guide followed along and noticed Jeff's hesitancy as they continued through the trees and to the bottom where the helicopter awaited. On their flight back up for a second run, the guide turned to Jeff and asked if he wanted some guidance. Realizing this person was far more of an expert in this area and feeling a little uneasy on the last run, he said, "Of course."

The guide said, "You are looking at the trees, and you need to look toward the white." Psychologists refer to this as *target fixation* by which the brain is focused on an object, and the person becomes unaware of their surroundings and ends up colliding with the object. Jeff's guide was telling him to look where you want to go versus where you don't want to go. During the next run, Jeff focused more on the white space and flew by the trees like they were not even around. Look at the solution or the destination versus the problem or the roadblock. This is a common strategy with cycling, motocross, and car racing as well. When you are barreling down the trail on a mountain bike and you see a rock in your path, the tendency is to watch the rock, so you avoid it. You want to look past the rock and to the route you want your front tire to go.

It is the same in business. While it is critical to understand the potential roadblocks, we cannot spend too much time dwelling on them. Psychotherapist Jonathan Alpert says, "When you focus on what you don't want, you tend to make that happen."[26] So focus on what you DO want.

Martin Seligman, the father of modern positive psychology, found that those who focus on the positives tend to be more successful than those who focus on the negatives. He has spent his career researching the differences between optimistic and pessimistic behaviors and how this thinking impacts results. In other words, do the people who see the glass as half full see higher results than the people who see it as half empty?

The pessimists see the world more like it is, while the optimists see the world better than it is. So the optimist is looking at the world through a slightly rose-colored lens. According to his research, that has significant benefits in work, health, and success.

In a study of head and neck cancer patients, optimistic patients reported a higher quality of life both before and after treatment, suggesting that their positive outlook buffered the effects of health-related distress. Similar findings of lower distress have been reported in individuals undergoing treatment for breast cancer.

Optimistic individuals also tend to be more aware of their health status and how to stay that way. Specifically, Radcliffe and Klein's (2002) research studied 146 middle-age adults and found that those with high optimism were more informed about heart attack risk factors, as well as the role of other risk factors on their health: stress, alcohol consumption, nutrition, smoking, fat consumption, and exercise. Studies have also shown that optimistic people were less likely to need rehospitalization after a coronary bypass or repeat cardiac operations (Scheier et al., 1999; Helgeson, 2003; Cauley et al., 2017). They were also less likely to develop high blood pressure than pessimists, suffer from stress-induced changes in immunity, and even develop heart disease.

At work, optimism has been linked to intrinsic motivation to work harder, endure during stressful circumstances, and show more goal-focused behavior (Luthans, 2003).

As an important contributor to employees' well-being, it has been linked to improved overall happiness in the workplace, task-orientation, solution-focused approaches, perseverance, and decision-making efficacy.[27]

Seligman looked at insurance agents for Metropolitan Life to see if optimistic agents outperformed pessimistic agents. At the time, Metropolitan Life focused their hiring practice on two variables: aptitude and motivation. Seligman added optimism to the screening process and "after two years found that optimistic employees had sold 31% more than the pessimists. Compounding this effect, candidates who failed the aptitude test and scored well on the optimism test did 57% better than the pessimists in the second year, suggesting that optimism played a more significant role than selling proficiency."[28]

We may think this is a fixed trait that you are born with, but Seligman says this is a learned behavior. According to Seligman, "The basis of optimism does not lie in positive phrases or images of victory, but in the way you think about causes," and this can be learned. When setbacks or failures occur, the pessimist sees this as normal and believes that if I have failed in the past, I will fail in the future, whereas the optimist sees it as a one-time event. To the contrary, in times of success or victories, the pessimists see it as a one-time event, whereas the optimists see it as normal and believes that since I have been successful in the past, I will be successful in the future. This is consistent with Carol Dweck's research on fixed versus growth mindset.

So if we can visualize a successful outcome, there is a greater chance we will reach that outcome than if we visualize failure. Your chance of success will grow even more if you are deliberate on where you focus your energy.

PLAN DELIBERATELY

While it is helpful to visualize your success, see the finish line, and be optimistic about your performance, you do have to do the arduous work.

PILLAR III — ITERATE

However, it should be the right work and part of a thought-out plan, so you optimize your energy and resources.

Just after I registered for the Tahoe 200, I spent many days figuring out what the next nine months would look like. While "running a lot" would definitely be part of this plan, it had to be more detailed, more specific, and targeted based on the time of year. I had to ramp up at a safe level, as too much running can quickly cause an injury, so balancing out with other exercises was critical. Given that some weeks called for over thirty hours of exercise, my caloric intake needed to rise accordingly or my body would eat away at the muscle, and I would lose too much weight. And with any endurance event, while it is critical to be in strong physical shape, people underestimate the mental component and are not prepared for how the mind will react.

I therefore broke my plan into three primary areas: 1) legs; 2) stomach; and 3) head. In essence, I needed to get into the best physical shape of my life, I needed to fuel my body with the optimal foods, and I needed to make sure I was mentally prepared for both the training and the race. I further broke down each of these segments. As a connoisseur of spreadsheets, I listed all the weeks down one column and then created columns for the number of miles or hours I would run or bike during that week. My wife, who is an exceptional cook and deeply knowledgeable on nutrition, developed a list of meals that would be optimal to fuel my body appropriately. I was eating the equivalent of five full meals a day, so this was helpful. From this and many aspects of the plan, I had a road map to follow. All this leads to being very deliberate about what you will, and equally important, what you will NOT, do. Once you have a high-level plan, further break down the tasks into more manageable chunks of work.

Remember Julie Cullivan, CIO of FireEye, and how she didn't let the obstacle of a nine-month deadline keep her from getting started on a

117

critical IT project? She motivated her team by reminding them that "we can't do it all at once so let's break it down into manageable chunks." In her head, she felt that since she likely would not have everything done in nine months, at least they would be partially done and would not be at zero then. She then told the CEO that it would be enough to move the company forward.

Julie is one of the finest "performers" I know. She can implement and execute a plan far better than most. She has worked with some people who have thrown out some wild ideas and each time thinks, "We are going to do what?" And over the years she has learned that you need a good mix of crazy and execution. She explained that "when someone throws out an idea, I do a lot of listening and let the Envisioners talk while I listen, so I understand the WHY. I don't immediately respond, so I can try and get in their moment and see what they see. My job is to understand why and then break it into measurable steps. And then we can agree on how we get there."

> "When someone throws out an idea, I do a lot of listening and let the Envisioners talk while I listen, so I understand the WHY."
>
> **Julie Cullivan**, former CIO of FireEye and CTO and CPO of Forescout Technologies

During the Plan stage, while assessing risk and obstacles, a tactic was to break problems down into smaller components. The same principle applies here, and that is to break big tasks into a smaller task. This does three things. First, it takes something daunting and turns it into a reasonable goal. Second, it allows you to have smaller celebrations and mini-rewards when you finish it. It feels good to complete something, even if small, so revel in that accomplishment. And third, it builds your confidence, which comes from repeated successes.

PRACTICE DELIBERATELY

Focusing in the right direction is great, especially when combined with targeted practice. Iterating is about being focused and deliberate on what you do to drive to your desired goal, as psychologist Anders Ericsson explored. Ericsson's original study looked at successful musicians studying at an academy and found that on average, the top performers had practiced for ten thousand hours by age twenty. That was an average of the participants despite there being a big spread among the musicians. Contrary to popular belief and Malcolm Gladwell popularizing the "10,000 Hours to Mastery Rule," Ericsson does not have a magic number, but he does say you have to practice a lot, and it is likely a big number. More important, be deliberate about your practice, which he defines as having "purposeful practice methods."

Practicing deliberatively involves setting specific and measurable goals. If you want to improve your golf game, you need to do more than go out and golf. You need to identify which aspect you are trying to improve, such as hitting the ball thirty yards further down the fairway or being more precise on the green. With each hit, you get immediate feedback to see how well you did and then evaluate what you can tweak to improve the next time.

Juliette Goodrich shared with me how practice, focus, and determination got her to her job as a CBS news reporter and then anchor. While in college, she interned at a TV station for a midsize market and fell in love with the business. Early on she set her sights to be a reporter in the much more competitive and top-rated market in San Francisco.

As Juliette told me, "In the news industry, you are only as good as your last story." When things did not go well, she would evaluate the tape, identify what happened, and then ask herself how she could improve. With TV and being able to get an instant replay of her performance, getting accurate and honest feedback was easy. It took many years to finally land a job as a CBS reporter in San Francisco after purposely going to several other smaller markets and working her way up the ranks. She did not fall into this job accidentally, nor does she believe people just fall into the right places. She worked hard, focused on her goal, and continued to hone her craft. But from the beginning, she had a plan, and she followed that plan.

Tom Brady had a plan to be an NFL starter even when he was the fourth-stringer when most teams only carried three quarterbacks on the roster. He was drafted in the sixth round by the New England Patriots with the 199th overall pick, yet he strove every day to get better, even with limited practice reps. In the *Sports Illustrated* article "Tom Brady's Forgotten Rookie Year,"[29] author Alex Prewitt recounts how Brady prepared for his opportunity even when he was left home on road trips. Several teammates were surprised he didn't get cut but saw how focused he was. "He'd always be out there throwing, running, everything," one said. "Every night he would go down to the basement and watch film, preparing like he was starting quarterback." Then, said another, "He'd get up so early and go to the stadium and watch film before anyone else got there."

Brady's response when they asked how he was hanging in there: "I can't control how much practice time I get, or how the guys in front of me play. All I can control is how much I study, what I do with the one or two reps they give me. And when my time comes, I'll be ready. Then, hopefully, the coach sees something he can work with, and then you are able to get your shot." *It wasn't until his second season in the league* that he got his shot, and he led the Patriots to an upset Super Bowl win. He's now been to the Super Bowl ten times and wears seven rings.

Early in my career, I was managing a small department with no budgetary responsibility. I knew I wanted to eventually manage a larger function and would need to demonstrate stronger financial acumen. At the beginning of the year, I created a budget, and each month I asked our finance department to pull my actuals so I could track our spending. My boss never asked for it, and the company was making so much money, it rarely was an issue if I overspent. I was frugal, so I rarely overspent. Being within budget was not a success criteria for my job at that time. But I knew that at some point it would be and felt it was good to practice when the stakes were low. A few years later, I had moved into a higher role in the organization and was managing a $14 million budget. Unfortunately, the market turned, the company needed to lay off staff, and budgeting became a priority. Every department head was asked to reduce their spending by 10 percent and needed to present their plan to the executive committee.

I presented three scenarios: 1) A 20 percent reduction, 2) a 10 percent reduction, and 3) a 0 percent reduction. The executive committee suggested a fourth option of a 5 percent increase. They had seen how valuable my function was to the company and how conscious I was with its money. I was one of the few departments whose budget stayed flat or increased that year. Practicing when it doesn't matter pays dividends when it does matter.

GET RID OF THE MUNDANE

My former CEO used to say that none of us works at maximum efficiency. It's true. We all have room to optimize.

Tim Weyland is accomplished in many areas. He is the vice president of human resources for a midsize technology company, an Ironman athlete, and a professional soccer referee who has officiated at the highest levels of the sport. He said it well, and he should know: "If you are going to be successful in something, you have to say no to other things." We cannot do everything great. When he is deep into Ironman training, he knows that he needs to move exercise higher on the priority list. Without too much difficulty, he says, he can find twelve hours in a week to get his training done. Initially you may think that is a lot, but it is only 7 percent of your week. Few of us operate at that level of efficiency. This involves getting rid of some tasks and routinizing others. When endurance coach and entrepreneur Paul Kinney advises people who are completing their first endurance event, he asks them, "What hobbies can you get rid of?" He then made this telling observation from all his years coaching people to reach the finish line: "People who manage their time well succeed."

There is a reason Mark Zuckerberg and Steve Jobs wore the same outfit every day. They wanted to focus their time and energy on more important things like running Facebook and Apple, respectively. Making decisions takes energy, so if you can reduce some of the lower-level decisions, you can have more energy for more prominent issues.

> "If you are going to be successful in something, you have to say no to other things."
>
> **Tim Weyland,** vice president of human resources for a technology company, Ironman athlete, and professional soccer referee

Barack Obama, as president of the United States, was a remarkably busy man. He—and I would say this for all presidents—did more than most of us do. In a *Vanity Fair* interview, Obama said, "You have to exercise, or at some point, you'll just break down." George W. Bush was the same and would often run six days a week. In addition to exercise, Obama emphasized that you also need to remove from your life the day-to-day problems that absorb most people for meaningful parts of their day. He mentioned research that shows the simple act of making decisions degrades one's ability to make further decisions. "You'll see I only wear gray and blue suits," Obama said. "I'm trying to pare down decisions. I don't want to make decisions about what I'm eating or wearing. Because I have too many other decisions to make...You need to focus your decision-making energy. You need to routinize yourself. You can't be going through the day distracted by trivia."[30]

Setting up routines or habits that can be replicated will save you time and energy in future projects. Some studies show it takes about thirty days to make something a habit. Granted, that will vary depending on the complexity and intensity of the task and how motivated one is to change. But it does take time. If you want to go to the gym every day, the first month is the hardest. Gym companies offer significant discounts and incentives in January after you binged on food through Thanksgiving and Christmas and realize you "want to get in better shape" or "lose a few pounds." They also know from years of being in business that most people will go for the first month but will not continue through February. And they still collect your money through the end of the year. If you can build into your routine a daily habit of going to the gym and survive the first month, your odds of making it through the second month improve. And if you already go on a regular basis and are frustrated with all the new members showing up on January 2, just wait a few weeks. Soon most of them will be back on the couch eating bonbons and not on your treadmill.

I knew that getting out of bed in order to ride on my bicycle trainer for one hour, eat a quick breakfast, and then go for a three-hour run every morning would not be easy. And when the alarm went off at 4:45 a.m., there were a lot of incentives to stay in bed. The more time it took for me to move from my pillow to my trainer, the more time I had to come up with an excuse for why staying in bed was the better option. It's cold outside. I'm tired. I didn't sleep well. My legs hurt. I have a lot planned for today. It looks like it could rain. And on and on and on.

So every night before I went to sleep, I would lay out all my clothes and gear needed for the morning's activities; place water bottles, nutrition bars, and a banana on the counter; and get my trainer ready. This was down to placing the TV remote next to my trainer so all I had to do was sit down, flip on the news, and spin. So from the time I stepped out of bed to the time my legs were spinning was less than five minutes.

Computer technology has also made it easy to save time. I recently raised $140,000 for a volunteer project I was overseeing. People would contribute online, an email would automatically come to me, and I would track the contribution. If I looked at each email when it came in and acted on it or kept it in my inbox, that would take time. So I created a rule that moved that email to a folder which I reviewed every few days. It saved me about twenty minutes a week. If I found two other areas like that, I just saved an hour. That may not seem like a lot, but it adds up over time, and eventually, like Tim Weyland, you will have found your twelve hours for the week.

What opportunities do you have to find twenty minutes a day?

GOOD ENOUGH IS GOOD ENOUGH

In 2000, I joined a software company after spending the first part of my career in a slow-paced, conservative financial services organization. Both companies were outstanding, but I learned to move faster when I moved into the technology space. While working on a project and revising my plan for the umpteenth time, my boss finally said to me, "Bryan, get it 90 percent right, and then we can tweak as we implement. We can't wait for the program to be perfect." He was teaching me how to iterate. It did not make sense to me initially, because why do something 90 percent right? I was designing a leadership training class and wanted to make sure that the first time a participant saw the class, it was perfect. There were several flaws in my argument.

First, perfection takes time, and the added time has diminishing returns. Sometimes 90 percent is good enough, and then you can tweak along the way. This is why your software programs or phone apps are always getting updates.

Second, perfection comes with a cost. Is the cost to get something from 99 percent optimal to 100 percent worth it? Even in what might make sense to get to perfection, it is not always good business. Ideally, we want the airplane we fly in to be perfect and for every system in it to work flawlessly. But they do not. Airlines are filled with redundancy. Most four-engine aircraft can fly with enough propulsion from just two engines. Redundancy is built into an airplane in case failure happens. Installing an extra engine on an airplane makes more business sense than building the perfect engine that would never fail.

Third, you are shutting off the ability to accept customer feedback. When you work hard to get something "perfect," by definition, customer feedback will not make a difference because it is already *as good as it can get*. The challenge is understanding what will acceptably exceed the customer's expectations in the time and cost for that customer.

And lastly, your expectations will not be met. How many times have you taken a project to perfection? For most of you, the answer is zero. For the rest of you, I am guessing a few are not being completely truthful. Congratulations, I guess. But ask yourself, was it really perfect?

This is how many technology companies see the world. Every software program has bugs, as there is never enough time to test everything.

I have managed two political campaigns in my life, which is far crazier than running two hundred miles. The first was a $323 million school bond campaign where I needed a 55 percent yes vote. The second was for a friend running for mayor of our eighty-thousand-person city where we needed a majority vote. You do not need to be 100 percent perfect to demonstrate success. In the first instance, I needed to be 55 percent perfect and the second one 50.1 percent perfect. There are three types of voters. First, there are those who will support your candidate or issue no matter what. Second, there are those who will support your opposition. And third, there are those who are undecided. You want to get all of your supporters out to vote and then focus heavily on getting the undecideds to choose you. If you try to be perfect and get every voter, you will spend way too much money and time on issues you likely won't change. Unfortunately, neither resulted in enough votes to be considered a success. If I had a fixed mindset, I would say I am not good at running elections and could never pass one. While my kids constantly remind me of my 0–2 campaign record, I just say that I have more to learn. It isn't that I can't win an election; it's just that I haven't…yet. The question is, Do I have a desire to do a third? At the moment, no. But if I do at a later date, I'll proceed by making adjustments based on my past experiences and additional research. I will have made it my WHY by determining whether it's important to me or to a cause—not because I need to prove to myself, my kids, or the world that I can do it.

DON'T SKIMP ON TESTING

When Howard Shao started Documentum with his cofounder John Newton, they were clear on their long-term goal but would reevaluate every six months. Along the way, Howard would learn, test, learn more, calibrate, then learn some more until they got it right. Anybody who works in QA and is responsible for testing will tell you that not enough time is spent testing. They will also tell you it is where time is compressed to get the product out the door. More likely than not, the product took longer to develop, and the salesperson sold to the original release date. Therefore, something has to give.

As Yvon Chouinard, famed mountain climber and Patagonia founder, said in his book *Let My People Go Surfing*, "You can minimize risk by doing your research and, most of all, by testing. Testing is an integral part of the Patagonia industrial design process, and it needs to be included in every part of this process. It involves testing competitors' products;

'quick and dirty' testing of new ideas to see if they are worth pursuing; fabric testing; 'living' with a new product to judge how hot the sales may be; testing production samples for function and durability, and so on; and test marketing a product to see if people will buy it."

Iterating is when you get to practice and find the flaws. It is about trying out new things and seeing how they work. Patagonia isn't the only one that tests their decisions—uh, products—before putting them in the real world.

I tried many pairs of shoes before I settled on the pair I wore at the starting line. Most endurance athletes will tell you to never try new equipment or nutrition on race day. Most of the trail in the Tahoe 200 is dirt and rock, causing your feet to be filthy after just a few miles. A friend had heard that spraying Pam cooking spray on your shoes beforehand will keep your feet cleaner. It sounded absurd, but she swore by it. Since dirt on the feet is a major cause for blisters, I thought I would test it out.

Months before and on a training run I started off with a brand-new pair of socks and shoes. On the right shoe, I sprayed Pam all over. The left shoe was my control group. After twenty-six miles of dusty trail, I sat down, took off both shoes and was amazed at what I saw. The left foot was a mess and brown. The right foot was as clean as when I left. Granted, it still smelled, but it was void of dust and dirt. I would never have tried this experiment on race day for fear of what could go wrong. Testing is about trying out things and making sure everything works as planned. When they do not, learn, calibrate, and test again. And when you test, it is good to have data to compare your results.

ACTIVITIES

QUESTIONS TO ASK YOURSELF

> What are the key tasks that need to be completed for each milestone?
> What smaller projects could you work on to improve your skills?
> What routines or habits can you develop to handle some of the routine activities?
> What intermediate goals will indicate you are on track and allow you to have shorter-term celebrations?

EXERCISES

> Incorporate one routine or habit into your week that will save you a total of one hour.
> Repeat the previous exercise.
> Write down two areas that you can deliberately work on to improve your chance of success.

Chapter 8

APPLY THE DATA

> "You get what you inspect, not what you expect."
> **Jeff Miller,** CEO, Documentum

I LOVE NUMBERS because they can tell so much. For me, they take the subjectivity out of an issue. For others, they get in the way of a good heartfelt decision. At some point, it is best to look at the numbers to see how you are doing using objective measures. They also help you change behavior. As my former boss would say, "You get what you inspect, not what you expect." The key is knowing what you should "inspect."

NOT ALL DATA ARE EQUAL

Reviewing the data involves 1) identifying the right metrics; 2) monitoring your progress along the way; and 3) adjusting when you find yourself off course.

How often have you heard someone say, "What information CAN

we measure?" That is the wrong question when it comes to identifying the right metrics. I often consult with leadership teams to help them develop their strategic plan and goals for the upcoming year. As part of this process, we also identify the right metrics to track our progress and evaluate success. As we start talking about the right measures, invariably someone will yell out, "It is easy to get data on…." Too often we pull the data that is easy to measure, when we should be asking ourselves, "What information SHOULD we measure to know if we are moving in the right direction?"

I was working with one organization that had recently acquired a smaller company. During this process, it became clear that some functions would need to be upgraded quickly. The quickest way would be to let some people go while hiring more skilled replacements to make this transformation.

The human resources department, not completely in tune with their internal client's need, was measuring and rewarding managers based on low employee turnover. In general, companies want low employee turnover but not in this case. They wanted to make sure the highly skilled employees didn't voluntarily leave. Instead of just looking at voluntary versus involuntary turnover, we started looking more deeply at the issue and broke those numbers down into "regrettable" voluntary turnover versus "desired" voluntary turnover. Let's be honest, there are some people who give their two-weeks' notice and you think, "It will be nice to see that person go," and then there are those about whom you think, "That's gonna hurt." Most human resource functions see those two people as the same impact when they report turnover rates to senior management. The key is to have several metrics that drive the desired results and don't encourage negative behavior.

What are the key metrics you should be watching to know if you are on track? In some cases, this is easy. For example, if you want to set a goal to lose thirty pounds in six months, you know you must average five pounds per month. Then, weigh yourself (at the same time of day) once per month and track your progress. If after month one you are only down four pounds, then you may need to adjust your program slightly. Sometimes the progression is linear, where you will lose five pounds in the first month, the second month, and on through the sixth month. If you are preparing for a marathon and you have to average twenty-five miles a week, your first week will likely only be ten miles. You need to start below your total weekly average and ramp up or you will overtrain in the first week and injure yourself.

The information we gather should provide us a context to make future decisions or course corrections. They should also define success in objective and measurable terms.

In my endurance events, I have generally identified three success criteria:

1. Good: Minimally acceptable. If it is my first time targeting this distance, this is often set to "just finish within the time limits set by the race officials."

2. Better: Reasonable stretch. As I am good at analyzing my performance and assessing what a reasonable finish time is, I usually set a faster target.

3. Best: Optimal result. This is often a major stretch and represents a situation if all things go close to perfect.

The Tahoe 200 was taking me into unchartered territories. In previous events, I had gone through one night with no sleep, but this would potentially take me through four nights with very little sleep. We had one hundred hours to complete the course, not including time cutoffs throughout the event. Early in my training I set the "Good" to be under one hundred hours, "Better" to be under eighty-six hours, and "Best" to be under eighty hours. I trained for "Best." As we entered July and with just under two months before race day, I did a forty-mile training run on the most difficult section of the course with a friend who had completed the race the year prior in eighty-six hours. As we finished, he turned to me and said eighty hours would be very doable, and I could potentially be a top-ten finisher. To be top ten would likely mean about seventy-five hours. I was ready.

So not only do you need to know the metric; you need to know how to assess your performance against that metric.

When Paul and Ilona Kinney were thinking of starting their own endurance coaching business in the San Francisco Bay area, they weren't sure what the market opportunity was like. They knew the weather in the area was ideal for outdoor activities. As they were in the heart of Silicon Valley, there were plenty of technology people with more disposable income than most communities and more flexibility in their schedule. As with any good entrepreneur, they found out the critical data points they had to evaluate and did their research. As Paul told me, "We believe in ourselves, but it is based on research." He went on to say, "In the beginning, I was worried the coaching business would be cyclical but then realized that it wasn't." Data helped to show them their coaching business was viable.

Remember Erik Molitor from the Envision pillar talking about how he made decisions that made his palms sweat in order to reach his goal? His goal, which he set early in his career, was to be a CIO before he turned forty. Given his background of graduating cum laude from a respected university, getting strong leadership development at GE, and having lived and worked overseas, he was clearly on the right path to being a senior executive. But his lofty goal still required him to go for jobs that may have seemed too big and pushed him outside his comfort zone. In his thirties, he became vice president overseeing several technology functions for a fairly large company. Knowing his forte is to gravitate toward technology and execution activities within his group, he knew he had to broaden his outreach to the full executive team. He told me, "I will measure myself on the amount of time I spend conducting outreach. If I measure myself today, this is probably only 5 percent of my time, but doubling it to 10 percent should be achievable if I focus on it and measure my progress monthly." Two months before his fortieth birthday, he accepted the role of CIO of a $3 billion medical technology company. He was focused, he knew what he had to do, and he tracked his progress.

MONITOR YOUR PROGRESS

For the Tahoe 200, I knew I had to achieve a certain number of biking/ running hours and miles per month. With today's GPS sports watches, it is easy to track. Those watches have more tracking features than one needs, from heart rate, average speed per mile, maximum speed, and over a hundred other data elements. And while I could easily pull all these data points, I didn't need that much information to focus on. Just because you can measure something doesn't mean you should.

With a nine-month training plan, I monitored my progress daily but evaluated my performance monthly. Part of my plan involved me running a consistent distance over four consecutive days once per month and increasing that distance each month. Early in the training this involved running ten miles on Sunday, Monday, Tuesday, and then finally Wednesday. The next month I ran four fifteen-mile days. Then four twenty, twenty-five, and finally thirty-mile days. So each month I could assess if I were on track and training to the level I needed. Since my race was in September, this meant the four thirty-milers took place in August during some of the warmer parts of the year. Adding in the heat while successfully accomplishing those back-to-back thirty-milers gave me a good indication if I was on track to run two hundred miles a month later.

When I managed human resource functions, we would have dashboards that allowed us to track the company's progress. We evaluated turnover, training, hiring, and costs, to name a few. If we wanted to get our attrition rate to a certain level, we knew that it may take a few years because of some systematic issues. We identified our current rate, assessed our ideal rate, and then determined a realistic time frame and strategy to close the gap. In this instance, we looked at the results quarterly to see if we were making progress.

Endurance paddler Matt Glerum used a GPS on his boat to see how changes in his paddling impacted his results and made him go faster and in a more direct route. He would ask, "What are the few things I could monitor that would have the greatest impact on my results?" He knew that if he watched a few key factors such as speed, heart rate, and perceived effort, he could get a feel of what would make him work better.

As business owner Liz Steblay, who we met in Chapter 3, says, "Anything that can be measured can be improved. So I measure everything, including how I spend my time in fifteen-minute increments. Every so often, I run a report to see if I'm investing enough time on business development, recruiting, or marketing. It's so easy to stay busy working in the business doing the day-to-day tasks. This is one way I make sure that I'm also working on the business, so it will continue to grow."

Chief Learning Officer George Brennan knows all too well about measurement. Early in his career and having just finished his PhD in organizational development, he was working for a large insurance company. The recently hired CEO wanted to create a culture that prioritized employee development and asked George to take this on. Changing a culture can take years, and George knew that he would have to show his boss that they were moving in the right direction.

Since insurance companies are all about data and employ a lot of actuaries who do this every day, George realized that he too would have to quantify his progress. He implemented several development programs early on and then added one question to the annual employee survey: "My manager cares about my development." For those managers who offered their employees the opportunity to attend those programs, they saw the response to that question go up 20 percent. Managers who didn't take advantage of the development programs didn't have an increase. George was changing the culture, and the executive staff was thrilled.

How often should you look at the progress? That is difficult to answer because like so many things in life, it depends. It is similar to how detailed your project plan should be. Do what works for you and your situation. For my training it was monthly, for the HR Dashboards it was quarterly, and for George Brennen's cultural change,

> "Anything that can be measured can be improved."
>
> **Liz Steblay**, founder and president of both PrōKo Agency and Professional Independent Consultants of America (PICA)

it was annually. However, with monitoring progress, you don't want it to be so frequent that it becomes onerous and doesn't add value. You also don't want it to be too spread out where if a problem occurs, you will find it difficult to recover.

Think of a pilot. Before taking off, they file a flight plan and review it throughout the journey. Pilots are constantly adjusting to make sure they are on their intended route. Wind, turbulence, jet stream, weather, and other aircraft can all move them away from the plan. They are constantly looking at this and adjusting as needed. If they waited hours, it may be too late and they may find themselves heading north to Canada when they wanted to go south to Mexico.

Monitoring your progress doesn't just have to be about graphs, dashboards, or spreadsheets. Matt, along with looking at hard data, used other factors to assess his performance. During his evening practice, he would monitor the sound of the paddle coming in and out of the water. He learned what an optimal stroke sounded like and could adjust accordingly. He would also watch how the light from the moon hit the bow of the boat to see if he was leaning too far one way. When you spend so much time working on something, you get a feel for what is working and what needs to be tweaked.

Try to have a visual that reminds you of your goals every day when you walk into a room. Career consultant Rob Delange has the goal to hike all fifty-eight "fourteeners" (peaks exceeding fourteen thousand feet above sea level) in the state of Colorado. Hanging in his home office above his computer is a map with all of them. Each time he summits, he puts a pin in the peak. Each morning when he walks in for his first meeting, that visual reminder keeps that goal at the forefront of his mind, which means it is more likely to get done.

Years before I took a career break and traveled for seven months around the world, I had a three-by-five-foot world map that hung on my wall. Hanging on a string from that map was a dry-erase pen I used to circle the countries I wanted to visit and write notes about getting from one country to the next. It constantly reminded me of my dream.

Whether you have hard data from a spreadsheet, a dashboard, or a map that hangs on the wall, identify the key element you should monitor to know that you are on track.

ACTIVITIES

QUESTIONS TO ASK YOURSELF

› How will you know you were successful and what measures will you use?
› What data points are needed to evaluate progress and your path to success?
› What areas should you monitor that will have the greatest impact on your progress?
› How frequently will you monitor your progress?
› What visual reminder of your dream do you have?

EXERCISES

› Identify two objective measures that you can track and will show your progress.
› Identify two to three success criteria in objective and measurable terms for your goal.

Chapter 9

MANAGE OBSTACLES AND RISKS

> "Growth and comfort do not coexist."
> **Ginni Rometty,** CEO, IBM

YOU MAY BE ASKING, didn't we already talk about obstacles and risks? Yes. Under Plan, we assessed the potential obstacles and risks that could impact our success and developed a plan to mitigate the chance they would happen. Now is when we implement that plan and deal with some of those obstacles as they come to be. That was PLAN…this is DO.

EXPECT PAIN AND MISERY

Obstacles will come, and you will face problems along your journey. That's normal. You should expect to feel pain or be miserable at some point. If you don't experience it, all the better. But rarely are big undertakings without some pain.

Every entrepreneur I spoke with knew there would be challenges and major obstacles. Some dealt with them when they arose, and some spent time eliminating the issue.

I know before I start a long bike ride or run that I too will experience both mental and physical challenges. In all these events, I generally break the distances into quarters. For the three-hundred-mile, twenty-four-hour bicycle ride, I see it this way:

1. Miles 0–75
2. Miles 76–150
3. Miles 151–225
4. Miles 226–300

The first quarter was easy, as my legs were fresh, the weather was cool, and I had done this distance many times in training. The second quarter was a little more difficult but still very doable, as I had also done this distance many times in training, and my body was used to the time and distance. The last quarter of the ride, while difficult, put me within view—figuratively, not literally for most of the way—of the finish line, and I could smell victory. Adrenaline pulled me through. It is the third quarter that is the hardest part for me. It generally occurs during the hottest part of the day (how do they plan that!) and I am only halfway done so can see neither the start nor the finish line, which are often the same location. I am often entering a distance I hadn't done during training rides, so my body is starting to experience fatigue. And did I mention I am only halfway done?

I recognize when I enter this third quarter that it is very normal for me to be tired, irritable, and not feeling great. I also recognize that this is normal, and I need to keep moving forward. I have experienced this same feeling at work when taking on a lengthy project, and at the beginning it is new and exciting. But as you get further into it and start experiencing roadblocks, whether political, financial, or technical, it gets to be tiring. When the end approaches, there tends to be a relief. Heck, I experienced it writing this book.

Being mentally prepared for the difficult times and knowing that they are normal will help when they actually do arrive. I will talk more about how to persevere through those difficult times in more detail under Perform. While it is good to be prepared for when the setbacks arrive, it is even better to reduce or eliminate the potential issues ahead of time.

REMOVE OR REDUCE POTENTIAL OBSTACLES

In talking with a woman who experienced many personal obstacles in her life, she relayed to me how she thinks of them like a video game. Do you remember playing *Pac-Man, Super Mario,* or *The Legend of Zelda*? In Level 1, the hurdles are small but then become more difficult as you progress forward. You easily fly through the early challenges, building your confidence. In some cases, you don't make it the first time but are able to on the second or third attempt. As you move into the higher levels, it may take more attempts to advance. Most of us start our life in Level 1 and experience Levels 2, 3, 4, and so on. Sometimes you may continue on to Levels 8, 9, and 10 in a certain area of life or work while others may stop playing and change games after Level 4. It all depends on the amount of excitement and motivation they have for the game, or life, that keeps them, or you, moving to that next adventure.

Tackling any big initiative adds stress, so the more you can reduce the known stressors, the easier it will be to navigate when the unknown stressors hit. If you are starting a business, there will be a period when your expenses will exceed your income. When you have a mortgage payment every month, small children to feed, or payroll to meet, that delta in your income may start to cause problems. You may find yourself focusing on that next mortgage payment versus that new feature in your software code or the meeting with a prospective investor.

Shane Kenny (who started up a software company), Justin Davis (who started up a coffee shop), and Andy Frey (who started up a mobile bike-repair business) all said the same thing. Make sure that you have enough money saved up to cover the living expenses to get through the tough times. All three were young entrepreneurs in their first business venture, and they did not want to worry about certain financial issues. Therefore, they eliminated or significantly reduced mortgage debt so they knew they could have a place to live even if expenses outpaced income. This reduced their spouses' anxiety as well. Never underestimate how your stress impacts others around you.

Along with being sound business and financial advice, it also is sound marital advice as well. When you are stressed, the first person to feel the pain is your partner. Paying off one's mortgage may be a bit of a stretch for some, but it is possible. While finances are often one of the larger obstacles or stressors faced, look at how you can minimize your anxiety and be able to sleep at night.

I have always loved the quote "Big problems are easy to see but hard to fix, while little problems are hard to see but easy to fix." Your job is to make sure you break those bigger problems down into smaller, more controllable chunks. Just like when you were developing your plan earlier and you broke the plan into smaller pieces, it is an equally effective way to handle large problems.

In Ben's real estate investment situation, he had one big worry: bankruptcy. You will recall, he broke that down into the three areas that would most likely cause this: 1) losing his day job; 2) losing a current tenant; and 3) having significant increase in renovation costs. He knew he could handle one of these issues occurring for a brief period of time, but if two—or worse, all three—occurred, it would cause substantial hardship. "To manage these," he told me, "I did some of the landscaping and construction work after my day job rather than pay someone else, I cut out expensive activities like concerts or plays, and I ate more tuna. I also kept thinking through the worst-case scenarios to figure out what I could do to mitigate those."

A lot of entrepreneurs learn to manage their finances tightly and often find themselves eating a lot of tuna or Top Ramen in the early days.

GIVE YOURSELF PERMISSION TO FAIL

CEO coach, venture capitalist, and former technology CEO John Hamm talked to me about how he deals with challenges along the way. As an excellent golfer, he has dealt with many obstacles before, often in the form of sand, rough, water, or trees. He shared with me that he deals with challenges in the boardroom the same way he deals with them on the links. He sets expectations early that he knows there will be problems along the way. He does not expect it will be easy or perfect and knows mistakes will happen. John told me, "I know during a golf game I will have a bad shot or two. So before the game, I say that I am allowed two bogies. I give myself permission for some mistakes. Not many, but some. If these occur in the first few holes, I can approach it in two ways. I could either panic and worry about it for the rest of the round, and lose focus, or I could say that those were my two allowable bogies and move on. I choose the latter." Every shot will not be the best one you can imagine, so permit yourself to fail, or as John says, "Take the boogeyman out of things and write it on the board that 'I will have x failures'—just say, publicly, what you know to be true.'"

If you are prepared for some failures, it won't take any energy from you. It is when you are not prepared that the energy is sucked from your body. This is not about ambition, or intention, it's about energy— it is a waste of energy to strive for unrealistic goals. As a VC and one who invests a lot of money in other people's ideas and companies, he fully expects some will fail. While any venture capital investor wants every one of their companies to succeed, they know there will be some disappointments.

> "I give myself permission for some mistakes. Not many, but some."
>
> **John Hamm,** former CEO, CEO coach, venture capitalist, and board member to several technology companies

Though it is good to AIM FOR perfect, it is unrealistic to BE perfect. I was talking to a woman who works in a midsize city, and she was tired of residents always complaining about some city policy and begrudgingly said, "You can't make everyone happy." My immediate thought was, "Are you trying to make everyone happy?" We can aim to make everyone happy or drive toward a perfectly executed project, but your expectations will likely not be met. Driving TOWARD perfection may cause unnecessary strain for an unrealistic result.

When I developed my nine-month training plan for the Tahoe 200, I was exercising six days a week. Early on, it was about two hours per day, then it increased to five hours per day. I knew there would be days I did not want to get out of bed and go for a run. When the alarm would go off at 4:45 a.m., and I could hear rain hitting the roof, it took every ounce of energy to move from my pillow to the front door. Knowing there would be days like this, I gave myself permission to "fail" or stay in bed and not exercise. As part of my training plan, I allowed three "free" days on which if I did not want to do anything, I could stay home. No questions asked. This did not include times I was injured and needed to rest; this was specifically for when I just did not want to go outside. Three days is not a lot over the course of 270 days, so I coveted these tightly. I remember one morning waking up and hearing a light rain outside and thought how nice it would feel to climb back under the covers. I then asked myself, "Do I want to use one of my golden tickets today and not have them in the future?" I got up, put on my running shoes and rain jacket, and walked out the door. That morning better prepared me when the rain started falling during the actual race.

As John Hamm and I have both found at times, giving yourself permission to not be perfect is a very freeing experience.

By the way, I never ended up using any of my three golden tickets. I don't say that to suggest my training was perfect—far from it. I simply mention that because giving myself permission to fail gave me motivation to push through the doubt and be better than I expected myself to be.

IF YOU MUST...BUT FOR THE RIGHT REASONS

Remember Matt Glerum, the endurance paddler? He is also a former CEO and extremely smart—MENSA smart. During college, he set a goal to get every question correct on every exam he took, which he did. As he approached the end of his college experience and having stayed diligently on track, he overslept one day and got a really good night's sleep. It felt great, which caused him to rethink his goals and measures of success. Goals change. Priorities change. And when that happens, adjust your measures. But first make sure you have the right measures to drive you to your definition of success. As Stephen Covey once said, "If the ladder is not leaning against the right wall, every step we take just gets us to the wrong place faster." You have permission to adjust your goals and move your ladder. But think back to the Envision section, and make sure you have the right reason and not some excuse—because it is hard, you are tired, or you aren't sure you can make it.

Matt learned early on how to do this. As an outdoorsman and adventure enthusiast all his life, Matt set a goal in high school to someday own a hunting and fishing lodge. He thought it would be the perfect career for him. After researching the skills needed, he realized that along with hunting and fishing acumen, he needed to know bookkeeping, marketing, and hospitality. Throughout college, he intentionally focused on jobs that would allow him to check off those skills. He worked his way from busboy to head waiter to floor manager. Toward the end of college, a client asked if he had math skills, then hired him to do accounting. Another box checked.

As he continued to learn more, Matt realized that lodge owners rarely get out in the field, which was something important to him. So he re-evaluated his goal and changed course. The learnings did not go to waste, as Matt went on to be an executive at several adventure and out-doors-related companies. Knowing when to keep moving down the road is critical, but then knowing when to adjust course is equally important.

When conditions change, ask yourself, "What is the real goal?" For Matt it was about being outdoors and fishing. Owning a lodge would not afford him that opportunity. He went on to a career and lifestyle that now allows him plenty of time to be standing in a river with a fly rod in his hand.

John Newton cofounded an enterprise software company that he sold before moving on to his next opportunity, where he had a decision to make. Having seen what massive success looks like, he was two years into his next company when the market took a turn. Customers left in droves, which moved the company in the wrong direction. While several of the key leaders and board members felt the company could regain its footing and move forward, others, including John, felt the risk pro-file was not worth the reward. He evaluated both the potential upside and downside. He looked at both the best-case and worst-case scenar-ios and felt there were other, more lucrative opportunities out there. He changed course.

Knowing when to pivot is not a hard-and-fast science. And while there is a lot of clear financial and risk analysis that should be calcu-lated, each person's understanding of that data will be different. Each person's comfort with risk will be different. And each person's tolerance for discomfort will be different. The challenge is knowing when to completely pivot or stop versus when to keep going. Recognizing there will be failures along the way is all about iterating. Why did James Dyson not pivot before his 5,127th prototype vacuum or WD-40 scientists stay the course after thirty-nine failures when others would have? They still felt it was doable.

There are many sound reasons to adjust course, but don't do it because you're looking for an easy way out.

ACTIVITIES

QUESTIONS TO ASK YOURSELF

> Of the obstacles you identified earlier, what will you do to manage them?

> Where have you given yourself permission to fail?

> What aspects of the situation do you have control or influence over?

> When do you expect the most pain and misery?

EXERCISES

> Write down what you will do to remove the stressors from your day-to-day life.

> Write down at least one area where you will allow yourself to not be perfect.

> Write down areas to manage or mitigate the pain and misery.

> Write down an area where you give yourself permission to fail.

PILLAR IV – COLLABORATE

> "Those who collaborate and improvise most effectively have prevailed."
> **Charles Darwin,** naturalist

COLLABORATE *with others and learn from*

experts. This involves learning from those who came before you so you can replicate their successes and avoid their setbacks. It is about having long-term advisors who help guide you through life and then preparing the people on your team who will ensure your success. Collaboration takes many forms, but most importantly you should remember that you can't go it alone to reach your goal. That is why it's significant to note that while Envision, Plan, Iterate, and Perform generally occur in that order, Collaborate occurs throughout.

SYNONYMS

TEAMWORK
SHARE
PARTNER
PARTICIPATE
CONSPIRE
COOPERATE
COMMUNICATE

When I am about to embark on anything big, I rely heavily on the people who went in front of me. Tahoe 200 was no different. Usually, for an endurance event such as a marathon, triathlon, or a century bike ride, you can type into Google, "Training Plan for _____" and get more results than you will need in less than a second. Millions of people—literally—complete these types of events every year. The New York City Marathon alone has over fifty thousand runners. Some plans are basic, with recommended mileage per week leading up to the race, while others are more thorough, with nutrition, mental exercises, and strength-training tips. It's a start.

Not many people have successfully completed a two-hundred-mile run, so the resources are far scarcer. But they exist. And fortunately, I happened to know two people who completed this same run the year prior. They are husband-and-wife ultradistance athletes Dan and Diann Boyle. She's also the former air force pilot who told me about the 6 Ps. I invited them for a run, asked them for advice, and listened. And that was just the beginning of my collaboration with this incredible couple.

I arrived at the finish line after seventy-six hours of running with the help of many people. During race weekend there were two crew chiefs (rotating so they could sleep) and five pacers. Take any one of those people out of the picture, and my ability to reach the finisher's arch is more challenging. Not impossible.

When a CEO of a company stands in front of a crowd to receive an industry award, they know full well, at least the good ones, that the award is the culmination of many people accomplishing their tasks. Most people I spoke with, upon recounting their successes, realized they put in a lot of work but also were successful because of those around them. Whether a supportive spouse, a trusted advisor, a collaborative colleague, or an understanding manager, there was someone who pushed, prodded, advised, and supported them along the way. Find these people.

Listen to these people. And most importantly, learn from these people.

BEHAVIORS (COLLABORATE)

The Collaborate pillar is broken into these three behaviors:

1. **Learn from others:** I seek advice from other people who have accomplished similar goals and include their learnings in my strategy.

2. **Cultivate key advisors:** I surround myself with people who either stretch themselves or encourage me to do the same as my longer-term advisors.

3. **Prepare your team:** I form a team that can support me in my endeavors and clearly outline to each of them what a successful outcome looks like.

Chapter 10

LEARN FROM OTHERS

> "The capacity to learn is a gift; the ability to learn is a skill; the willingness to learn is a choice."
>
> **Brian Herbert**, author

TOO MANY PEOPLE THINK that their "situation is different" or "so unique." We are good at looking at the differences, and while there are surely variations between your situation and that other person's, I urge you to focus on the similarities and glean information about those aspects. Then adjust their plan to meet your differences. We live in a technological world built on crowdsourcing information on just about anything, and that allows us to reach out directly to experts. It has never been easier to collaborate. Why put yourself at a disadvantage by trying to go it alone when answers are there that will help you excel faster and better?

SOLO COLLABORATION...IT'S A THING

Oscar Wilde said, "Imitation is the sincerest form of flattery...." I am not suggesting you illegally copy someone's proprietary work, but there is enough free stuff available to get you started. A friend of mine was getting married, and she was feeling a bit harried, as she didn't know where to start the planning process. I suggested she Google "Wedding Project Plans" and find one that is consistent with what she wanted to accomplish. She did, and it got her started.

The same is true for other types of plans. Want to start a business? Build a website? Implement SAP? Plan a reunion? Remodel your house? All of these have complex plans available, and while they may not be exactly for your situation, they are a start and may offer some good direction.

The amount of information at our fingertips is extraordinary. As a kid, I remember going to the library and pulling out one letter of the *Encyclopedia Britannica* and turning to a page. If I wanted to learn about Mars, I would look for the "M" book and flip through the pages. There were a few paragraphs about the red planet. To learn more, I would have to dig deeper into the archives and find books. Some of you may recall sorting through the card catalogue to find the Dewey decimal classification, at which point you would go hunting for the book on the shelf. And if you were lucky, it was available. It may have taken fifteen minutes to find that one book.

Now I watch my kids do their research from their bed. They can download a book onto their Kindle from the library, pull up a magazine or the *New York Times* on their iPad, listen to a podcast on their iPhone, or conduct a Google search on their computer. Of course, they also get distracted from that research by scrolling through TikTok and posting on Instagram, but the point remains: you can learn a lot about anything you desire with a few clicks. Many years ago, I read a quote that said, "If you read today's *New York Times* cover to cover, it would contain the same amount of information that a person in the fifteenth century would have learned in a lifetime." We are deluged with information, and it is extremely accessible from wherever we are. That's good and bad.

This type of research is what fitness executive and Ironman Ralph Rajs referred to as "solo collaboration." It's something he does all the time before starting anything big. I thought it was an oxymoron, as this section is titled "Collaborate," which *Merriam-Webster* defines as "to work jointly with others or together especially in an intellectual endeavor."[31] I asked Ralph—"How can you collaborate by yourself?" Ralph replied that collaboration was not his forte, but he realizes how critical it is in today's world. To learn from the experts, he reads a lot of blogs, books, or magazines. So instead of talking to these experts through synchronous collaboration, he is gathering their expertise asynchronously.

Within seconds you can have a marathon training calendar or sample business plan on your computer ready to customize for your situation. According to PodcastHosting.org, in 2020 there were over one million podcasts and over twenty-nine million episodes.[32] And they cover every possible subject out there, ranging from art to zebras. Chances are you will find something tied to your needs.

COMPETE AGAINST PEOPLE SLIGHTLY BETTER THAN YOU

"Scientists have found that head-to-head competition against someone slightly faster than you results in faster performance for you in about 80 percent of the cases,"[33] according to Florentina Hettinga, professor in the Sports, Exercise and Rehabilitation Department at the UK's Northumbria University. "It can help you become as much as 2 percent faster." In another study done at the same university, cyclists raced against an avatar. The cyclists were told the avatar was moving at their personal best speed when the avatar was moving 2 percent faster. The cyclists kept up with their virtual competitor.

As the research showed, racing against someone slightly better than you will often result in you going faster than you had in the past. A good friend of mine is a phenomenal downhill runner. He will beat me on most descents, but I became a better downhill runner because of him despite him winning most times. We would both push each other down the hill to the point I felt like the top half of my body was starting to move faster than the bottom half, which could result in a bad fall—it never did.

The more we ran, the faster I got, and the amount of time he waited for me at the bottom became less and less. For those rare instances I inched ahead of him, I also knew that I was making him faster as well. However, if your competition is so much better that it's no contest, then you may become disheartened. Do you really think playing H-O-R-S-E with Stephen Curry or racing Usain Bolt over a hundred meters is going to do you any good?

People often see the negative aspects of competition and how it pits one person against another, resulting in a winner and loser. My wife, who is the kindest soul in the universe, often cringes when I suggest a family competition. During COVID, I suggested we do a Family Iron Chef where three of the four members are responsible for cooking part of the dinner while the other judges. My goal wasn't to prove who was the best cook between the four of us—my wife clearly is—but to have everybody bring their A-Game and raise the bar for all the competitors.

At our first competition, my oldest son—thirteen at the time—made calamari from scratch, and he had to clean and prepare the squid. It was fantastic and better than any restaurant I've been to. He raised the bar that day for all of us and made me realize that I have to do better. The next time, my younger son—nine at the time—made coquilles Saint-Jacques and raised the bar even higher. I was never so happy to lose because both kids stepped up and pushed everyone to do better—including themselves. They deserved the win.

If you are always the strongest person in the competition and routinely win, you will feed your ego, but you won't significantly enhance your skill set. I was talking to a competitive youth soccer coach who often would scrimmage his team against boys who were a few years older. He wanted to push his kids to rise to their potential and play up a level. Even though they would lose more often than they would win against that team, they played at a higher caliber than when they played kids their own age. And when they played kids their own age, they won most of the time.

THE SECRET IS TO LIMIT MIRACLES

NASA is sending a drone to Saturn's largest moon, called Titan. This could provide clues to how life started on earth. The dual-rotor quadcopter, Dragonfly, needs to be completely autonomous because it is so far from the earth and there is no way to recharge the batteries. Doug Adams, the mission's spacecraft systems engineer, says that "almost everyone who gets exposed to Dragonfly has a similar thought process. The first time you see it, you think: 'You gotta be kidding—that's crazy.'"[34] But the engineer goes on to make a series of quotes that show it's not crazy at all:

> ＞ "The mission is possible using technology we use all the time on earth."
> ＞ "Quadcopter technology is all over the place, but this one is just a little bit bigger."
> ＞ "Self-driving technology is increasingly common."
> ＞ "It should be easy on Titan as there aren't any obstacles."

Recharging the drone is the biggest problem, but they learned from another industry: nuclear submarines. They also learned from other missions, such as trips to Mars, that require battery technology.

One of the strategies to reduce risk is to use proven technology and learn from other people, other companies, or other industries. Adams goes on to say that the "secret is to limit miracles. We are assembling as many technologies that are already existing as possible." Whether you are flying a quadcopter to one of Saturn's moons or taking on a new challenge, there is someone who can help.

Tracy Coté, chief people officer (CPO), knows firsthand. As she was getting ready to take on a much bigger role as the CPO for a two-thousand-person company with twenty staff members around the world compared to the three-hundred-person company with four staff members all in the same office, she realized she needed help. It was a big job, and she had doubts about her ability to successfully do the job. With little international experience, not only was Tracy taking on a riskier role, but the company was also taking a chance on her, and she did not want to let them down. "I didn't know a lot about M&A, global HR practices at scale, and more, so I asked the outgoing CHRO to consult with me for a period of time, having her tackle a few big projects while offering insights and advice as needed as I immersed myself in the role."

Asking for help is unfortunately seen as a weakness in our society. And you may feel like you are burdening the other person. It only seems that way to the person asking for help. Most of the time, the person being asked sees it differently.

First, regarding weakness. Are you the de facto expert? Could someone know more than you? Could you learn from them? We are not great at everything. No one expects us to be great at everything. We have weaknesses, deficiencies, and gaps in our knowledge. That's OK. That's normal. That's human. Granted, if you are the head of finance and you ask your head of marketing to explain basic financial terms, you (and your organization) have a big problem. But that's an extreme example. You are expected to know your domain, although you still can likely learn from others about your specialty. If that same finance exec is taking a company public for the first time, she would be well served to seek guidance.

Second, on being a burden. Chances are you are not and will likely flatter the person you ask. Think of the last time someone looked to you for guidance. Did you feel it was a burden?

I often provide career advice to kids coming out of college, and I give them the same information I was given when I was in their shoes. Find people in the industry or type of job you are interested in. Then ask them for a twenty-minute informational interview to learn about what they do and how they got into that line of work. They will appreciate your gumption in reaching out and want to help out the next generation. Most will realize that at some point they were in those shoes and now have the opportunity to help out. And most can find twenty minutes, even though it will likely turn into a much longer discussion.

Coincidentally, when I was leaving college and conducting interviews in 1991, I reached out to someone I knew about an informational interview. He worked in San Francisco and took me out to lunch at a nice restaurant. When I offered to pay, he said, "I've got it, but make sure to pay it forward." Twenty-one years later when I was looking for my replacement as VP of human resources, his resume came across my desk. We hadn't been in contact for years, and I called him up and repaid him for that informational interview. He now holds my former position.

For all my interviews for this book, and I was asking for one hour of their time, I only had two of the more than one hundred people I talked to say no. Both had very legitimate personal reasons why they could not talk at this time. Everyone else was happy to help. Why? Because I was asking about them. And who doesn't want to talk about themselves? But before you meet someone, do your research so you can maximize your time together and ask pointed questions.

ACTIVITIES

QUESTIONS TO ASK YOURSELF

> Who has done something similar to what you are looking to do?
> How is it they were successful?
> What barriers or obstacles did they overcome?
> What blogs, podcasts, trade associations, groups (online or in person), or other materials exist around this subject?
> What questions should you ask to learn more about the subject?
> What plans or templates have already been created that you can customize for your situation?

EXERCISES

> Identify five people who have achieved a similar goal whom you could interview.
> Write down five places you can go to learn more.
> Find someone who is slightly better at this task than you are and work with them.
> Choose one of the top people in the world in your area of interest and land an informational interview with that person.

Chapter 11

CULTIVATE KEY ADVISORS

> "Find a mentor who believes in you; your life will change forever."
> **Bill Walsh,** coach, San Francisco 49ers

WHILE IT MAY APPEAR "Learn from others" and "Cultivate key advisors" are the same, the fundamental difference is that when you are learning from others, that is for a specific project, initiative, or goal. At this point you have identified your goal, and the focus is on how to achieve it. With key advisors, these people should be considered long-term mentors. They could come from a wide variety of industries or positions, from spiritual leaders, counselors, and life coaches to content experts, trusted friends, and community leaders. In truth, the titles are not important; their knowledge of you and your goals and values, as well as a willingness to be honest and real with you, is. While at times they may advise you on a specific goal, they have a much longer time frame and a broader perspective.

These people have wisdom, a unique perspective, or a wider view of a situation. They may be a former boss whom you rely on for career advice or strategic guidance and meet with every few months, a colleague you respect who may be a step or two ahead of you in their career, a friend who pushes you a bit further than you would normally go, or an advisor who helps you see something in a different light. As Chief People Officer Tracy Coté

> "You have to find the right people to speak with you about your ideas and challenges. A friend, mentor, maybe even your mom, but someone who will let you think out loud and not put you down while they help you explore solutions in a nonjudgmental way."
>
> **Tracy Coté,** chief people officer

told me, "You have to find the right people to speak with you about your ideas and challenges. A friend, a mentor, maybe even your mom, but someone who will let you think out loud and not put you down while they help you explore solutions in a nonjudgmental way." Every public company has a board of directors who have a diverse level of expertise and knowledge. This is YOUR board of directors.

USE YOUR NETWORK TO MOTIVATE YOU

There are times you ask people for feedback, and you genuinely want to know. Even if it is ugly, you want to know. There are also times you just want validation. Let's be honest: you've surely asked someone for their input when really you just were hoping they would say, "Yeah, it looks good." I have one friend who whenever I give her something to review, she is going to give highly constructive feedback. She assumes that if I did not want to know, I would not have asked, and she is not afraid to respond. She is direct. She is clear. And, most importantly, she is highly

2324

225382

288

knowledgeable in the areas I ask about. If I have something that I think is 90 percent correct, and I need validation, she is not the person. But she will get me to 98 percent.

If I am looking for validation, there are other people I call on. You know, like your mother. Well, I don't know your mother, so maybe I should steer clear of that suggestion and let you handle your own family dynamics.

I have a friend who will always say something positive no matter how bad the work I give him is. If my self-esteem is feeling a bit low about something I am writing, he can make me feel like William Shakespeare when the quality is slightly better than that of a first-grader.

Let me state it another way. It is January and you've just survived the holidays. Instead of reducing calories by working out on the treadmill, you find yourself overindulging at all those holiday parties. And while feeling a little overweight, you ask your spouse, "Do I look fat?" Deep down, are you really looking for an accurate answer? To all the men: if you have any doubt about how to answer this question, let me offer you some guidance, as there is only one correct answer and that is, "No, honey, you look beautiful." Do not pause after the question and think about it; answer quickly and confidently, then change the subject. You will regret any answer to the contrary.

So be clear in your mind whom you rely on for feedback and why you need it. Do you need a little motivation to keep you moving forward or do you need help resolving a problem you can't figure out?

> "I have about four people in my life who I trust and will tell me the truth."
>
> **Aaron Kenny,** cofounder of InternetSafety.com, CTO, and entrepreneur

Entrepreneur Aaron Kenny says, "I have about four people in my life who I trust and will tell me the truth. They will tell me if an idea is crazy, help me understand the market better, and advise me on business issues and how much time something may take." Aaron believes a big part of his success is because of these trusted advisors.

SURROUND YOURSELF WITH OTHER ~~CRAZY~~ COURAGEOUS PEOPLE

Doing amazing things is often a part of who someone is. Many people I interviewed said, "I don't have much to add," because they did not see their accomplishments as quite amazing. Becoming a CXO or completing an ultradistance event is NOT common for most people, but for these people it is. Every week, I run with a group of friends where everyone has either run fifty, one hundred, or two hundred miles, biked one hundred miles, or completed an Ironman. Some have dived with sharks, jumped out of airplanes, and flown military jets. When you hang around people like this, your perspective on the ability to accomplish amazing things may be a little off. It is why when someone says to me, "I could never do…," I am skeptical because I have seen and talked to so many people who did "do…."

If you surround yourself with people who like to sit around and watch television, you will find yourself watching a lot of TV. If you surround yourself with people who push themselves and try new things, guess what? You will push yourself and try new things.

Peer pressure is often associated with negative aspects such as high school friends encouraging you to try drugs or a friend telling you to drive a little faster. But there is a positive element when these same friends or coworkers encourage you to try good things.

Think of a time you worked with a high-performing team that kept raising the bar and pushing the limits versus when you worked with a group that stuck to the status quo and did what had always been done. When did you perform your best, and when were you most excited in your job?

The people I spoke with performed at a higher level when others around them encouraged that type of behavior. And in many cases, they performed at a higher level when they surrounded themselves with people better than they were. Never underestimate the value to your well-being and your community that is created when you invite supportive and committed people into your sphere of influence.

What type of people are you hanging around?

SOMETIMES IT'S OK TO IGNORE ADVICE

Collaboration is all about listening to others. It is also about knowing when to heed the advice and when to follow your own expertise. Alicia Wallace, All Across Africa, has used mentors a lot to build her business to include five thousand weavers. She has listened to and evaluated their feedback and, in many cases, followed their guidance. But as she told me, "Don't blindly trust."

Sometimes you have to say no to feedback and trust your own instincts.

One month before I was set to start my four-thousand-mile bicycle ride across the United States, the guy who was to go with me backed out. It was a legitimate reason, as his father was diagnosed with cancer. I was faced with the decision of going by myself at the age of twenty or pushing the trip off to the following summer. These were the days before cell phones, GPS tracking devices, and Find My Friends, making it nerve racking for my mother to wonder where I was.

"Don't blindly trust."

Alicia Wallace, cofounder and chief operating officer, All Across Africa

A few days after my friend had to back out, a relative connected me with two other guys who were planning to cycle across the US at about the same time and suggested I join their group. Everybody was telling me

I should go with these guys, including family, friends, people I trusted, and fellow cyclists. But I thought it prudent to meet with them to determine if this could be a good option.

After spending a few hours with these other cyclists, I realized it was not a good match and even questioned if they would be successful. I already had many long-distance cycle tours under my belt; this was their first. When I heard their plan and their experience, I was not confident they would make it to the East Coast and did not want to be part of an unsuccessful team.

I told my trusted advisors and family about my decision, and they did not show the disappointment I knew they felt. About two weeks after I started, I received word that the other guys quit after ten days. It was harder than they imagined, and they were not prepared. I tend to be very analytical, but sometimes you have to trust your gut.

ACTIVITIES

QUESTIONS TO ASK YOURSELF

> Who are your mentors or advisors?
> Who are the people you rely on to pick you up when you are down?
> Who can provide you honest and helpful input or feedback?
> Who in your life regularly pushes you outside your comfort zone?

EXERCISES

> Identify what you are looking for in a long-term advisor.
> Identify, then ask, two to three people who could act as your long-term advisors.

Chapter 12

PREPARE YOUR TEAM

> "We may not be right, but we're not confused."
> **Jeff Miller**, CEO, Documentum

As CEO, one of Jeff Miller's primary responsibilities was to figure out what direction to take the company. Should he shift the strategy or stay the course? The day after the quarterly earnings call and seeing the stock drop 30 percent, Jeff was in front of the company explaining what happened. Wall Street was expecting more. Jeff was evaluating when and what changes he should make. And as he stood in front of the thousand employees, he talked through the strategy. He made sure the strategy was clear to everyone and that we were all moving in the same direction. It is hard to know if the strategy is right, but while he had confidence in the direction, he wanted to make sure every one of those thousand employees who were listening to him was also very clear on the direction and their role. "We may not be right, but we're not confused" was his motto. Jeff recognized that choosing the right strategy is often difficult, and you may experience headwinds not within your control. But what you do control is if everyone is aware and aligned around the strategy. Or, as Jeff also says, "Any team 100 percent focused on an 80 percent correct strategy WINS!" Alignment gets you to your destination faster, so even if your strategy is imperfect, you will realize it quicker and be able to pivot.

Years earlier, when Howard Shao, John Newton, and Razmik Abnous started that company and before they hired Jeff to be CEO, they each had about twenty years of experience—all quite different but complementary enough to move their idea forward. Razmik told me, "I believed we weren't crazy because Howard and John put an amazing team together, and if it weren't for the three of us and a few we hired in the beginning, the idea would never have happened." This was a common theme among the people I interviewed.

Kevin Chou, founder of gaming company Kabam, grew his company from a business plan to $400 million in annual revenue. When I talked to him, he was on his second company and said, "I've gotten better at building teams who can perform. I have stronger execs who are better at the planning and tactical iterations. For second-time founders, it is easier."

All of these founders were extremely bright people and knew their technology and business better than anyone. But they were also smart enough to know they couldn't build their company alone. So they joined forces and built a powerful team.

BUILD AN ALIGNED AND COHESIVE TEAM

Ernest Shackleton, in his quest to pull together his team of fifty explorers for the Imperial Trans-Antarctic Expedition, supposedly posted the following ad in the paper:

HELP WANTED

MEN WANTED for hazardous journey, small wages, bitter cold, long months of complete darkness, constant danger, safe return doubtful, honor and recognition in case of success.

Not your typical job posting nor one that would build confidence in anyone applying, but it worked. Five thousand people applied for the fifty available slots.[35] And like many of the executives I spoke to, Shackleton didn't hire just on technical expertise but those who met his values of optimism, patience, imagination, and courage. It is amazing what people will do when there is an exciting and compelling mission.

Most startups have very little capital and can't pay a comparable salary to their much bigger counterparts. So for Startup X to attract a candidate against Microsoft, Facebook, or Google, they need to put together a compelling argument. They attract people by having a chance to build something new, work on cool technology, or an opportunity to make a boatload of money through equity. They may not be able to offer a stable salary but often attract people on a quest to be part of something even bigger.

I was consulting with one small to midsize technology company who was considering a move into downtown San Francisco so they could attract the young millennials that Google or Facebook were attracting. This company had engineers who were in their thirties and forties with kids at home. They didn't want to live in the city where the commute would be much longer; they didn't want to work eighty to a hundred hours per week. They didn't care about three free meals a day, as they wanted to be home for dinner with their spouse and kids and then log in after dinner to finish a project or respond to some emails.

If they were to move into the city, they would have to offer the same perks those other companies were offering, such as free lunches, shuttles, and game rooms. But they weren't going to pay for that. I suggested leaning into what made them different and understand their employees' wishes. Then put a compelling proposition for those types of employees to join and stay. We all have different reasons for joining an organization, team, or endeavor; your job as the leader is to understand that WHY and attract THOSE people. They didn't move.

Not everyone wants to be part of one person's quest to run two hundred miles, but there are those who think it is the coolest thing. Several months before Tahoe, I needed a half dozen people to help me to the finish line. They wouldn't receive a finisher's medal or get to wear the T-shirt. They would, however, have to endure long hours of running at whatever time I needed them, and have to deal with a potentially whiney, tired, irritable runner. And for what? In some instances, they would have to wake up at two in the morning, drive an hour to a remote location, and wait for a few hours until I arrived, changed my socks, and then left to the next aid station. On paper, it seems like a terrible job and may seem hard to get people. But that purpose of being part of something bigger is an aspect many can't turn down. My job was to get people excited.

Pacers and crew were a necessary part of my team and had a daunting and thankless job. But when all was said and done, it was easy to convince five pacers and two crew to join in my adventure. They each had their reasons, as did I. They trusted me to work hard and hold up my end of the bargain. That trust raised my confidence in being able to finish. They also unknowingly pushed me because I was motivated to reach the end not just for me, but for them. They didn't want to let me down. But I also didn't want to let them down. So "quitting" never became an option.

Rarely do we do things alone. Even sports that appear to be individual rely heavily on a team. People often think professional cycling is an individual sport. In the Tour de France, each team consists of nine riders: one is the leader, or captain, and the others support that person to win. They are referred to as "domestiques." If the captain gets a flat, the others give up their bike and wait for the team car. Domestiques will lead out in front blocking the wind while the captain drafts. And when one domestique gets tired, another will take his place. When you set a lofty goal, find people whom you can work with, rely upon, and trust to take you across the finish line.

Ironman and adventure athlete Ralph Rajs learned a valuable lesson early on in his competition. He was competing in a twenty-four-hour adventure race as part of a three-person team—all accomplished and all with sponsorship money behind them. Unfortunately, during the race they missed a time cutoff, ending their race. Ralph was devastated because along with each teammate leaving their families to participate in this race and putting up a lot of their own money in addition to sponsors' money, they didn't come close to their goals. After assessing the failure, he realized "1) we trained differently; 2) we weren't prepared; and 3) we weren't aligned around our commitment and success of the race." Remember what Jeff Miller said: "We may not be right, but we're not confused." Unfortunately, they were confused, and it became a valuable lesson Ralph relayed to me. It never happened again.

In contrast, Matt Glerum, CEO and adventure paddler, pulled together his six-person team for

> "Now that we are clear we want to be a top finisher, this changes the training strategy and commitment required by each person."
>
> **Matt Glerum,** CEO of TravelSmith Outfitters and ZoomSystems, entrepreneur, and adventure paddler

the epic Yukon River Quest and aligned on the team's goals before dipping the paddle into the water. The 444-mile race goes down the Yukon River, from Whitehorse to Dawson City, Yukon Territory, Canada. As Matt shared some of the early discussions the team had, it became very clear they were out to be a top finisher and not just have a good time. Matt said to me, "Now that we are clear we want to be a top finisher, this changes the training strategy and commitment required by each person. But we also wanted to have fun and have people in the boat who will make us laugh." Their early discussions, alignment around goals, and focused training paid off with an impressive place on the podium. Unlike Ralph's team, Matt's team was aligned around their goals.

MAKE SURE THEY ARE READY

As I prepared my crew for Tahoe, I pulled everyone together a month before the race. I reviewed the course, the race rules, and the expected challenges. We walked through "What if…" scenarios and what my role was, what my crew members' roles were, and what my pacers' roles were. In essence:

> Runner (Me): Eat and keep moving forward.
> Crew: Get me out of the aid station.
> Pacers: Get me to the next aid station.

If each of us played our role, we would all celebrate 205 miles later at the finish line.

We also talked about who had the authority, outside the race officials, to pull me from the event. If it became too dangerous for me to continue, I gave my crew chief complete authority to say, "Bryan, you're done. Get in the van and we are going home." If it got to that point, I knew I wouldn't be the best person to make that decision and needed someone who was more coherent and rational to make that call. Fortunately, we never had to cross that bridge.

As CEO of multimillion-dollar company, Bill Wheeler realized that it was difficult for him to take off and travel for extended periods of time unless his executive team could handle it in his absence. Difficult, not impossible. As an avid adventurer, he told me he had to "prepare the team to manage the business when I was away. So I designed the systems to be away from the office." He successfully did this many times over the course of a seven-year period when he took off for a few weeks at a time while he rode his motorcycle around the world through Central and South America, Southeast Asia, and Mongolia. It is also helpful as he regularly travels abroad to deliver some of the ten thousand wheelchairs in twenty-one countries as part of the Wheelchair Foundation through Rotary.

One person I spoke to was asked to turn around a failing company. He couldn't resist an exciting challenge. He told me, "My goal was to rebuild the company and move it into profitability, and I focused on two areas: 1) my team and 2) my suppliers." He considered his suppliers an extension of his team. Over a short period, he made significant progress and eventually quadrupled sales and turned it profitable.

It is good to prepare your team and align around the priorities. Have these conversations early when everyone is happy and can talk in a reasonable manner. In my years coaching teams, I advise the same. Set ground rules early, talk through how to handle difficulties, and align around priorities. Because, when the shit starts to fly off the fan, rational minds do not prevail. These early discussions will improve your odds of a sounder solution being implemented and make sure you are ready to perform.

ACTIVITIES

QUESTIONS TO ASK YOURSELF

› What do you need from other people to succeed?

› What will get them excited to participate?

› When problems occur, what support will you need?

› What is the role each person plays?

EXERCISES

› Ask two to three people if they would be willing to help and explain what you need.

› Clarify what success looks like to all involved.

PILLAR V – PERFORM

"There is nothing more rewarding than accomplishing something you were too crazy to start in the first place."

Steve Sherman, Ironman

PERFORM

to your plan and persevere to the finish line. You are now standing at the starting line. Your training and preparation should set you up to reach your goal. While this is one of the shorter pillars, it is because you have already done the hard work, and you are ready to shine. But getting to the finish line still requires you to overcome some difficult times.

SYNONYMS

DO IT

FOLLOW THROUGH

ACCOMPLISH

EXECUTE

COMPLETE

IMPLEMENT

FULFILL

ACHIEVE

EVENTUALLY, YOU WILL FIND yourself at the starting line waiting for the gun to go off. If it is your first time, then you are surely nervous. If you're not nervous, are you being honest with yourself?

In many ways, getting here is the hardest part. The seventy-six hours between the start of my 205-mile run and the finish was far easier than the year of preparation. People often ask me the most difficult parts of this event. "The training," (Iteration) I say. If you have followed your plan, done your homework, and prepared, your day will go better than the person's who didn't. If, during training, you woke up at 3:30 in the morning and ran in the rain or in the middle of the day when it was a hundred degrees, you will do better when those conditions hit compared to the person who slept in. You will still experience challenges, but those hurdles will be easier to get over.

STANDING AT THE STARTING LINE

As we learned from Seligman's research on optimism, our chance of success will increase if we believe we will be successful. But you must do more than believe, as success requires a lot of hard work.

While Iterate is taking a long-term goal and breaking it down into shorter, more manageable goals, Perform IS the long-term goal. For example, if you want to climb Mt. Everest, you don't start in Nepal. You iterate and climb smaller, local mountains in your region in more temperate climates. And then you work your way up to more difficult terrain and in more treacherous conditions. You increase your skill set over time. Then you Perform by climbing Everest.

One entrepreneur I spoke to has a long-term goal of being a founder and CEO of a social enterprise in Guatemala. He estimated it was five to ten years out, but in the meantime, he was building up his business skills with smaller projects, developing his network, and working in the nonprofit space. CEOs don't start as CEOs.

Many years ago they were individual contributors then managers, then directors, then vice presidents. They may have started in one function but then got experience in sales or marketing or finance or operations until they had solid general management skills. It takes time. Remember, the person who makes the most in a Get Rich Quick scheme is the person who invented the scheme. Sustained success more often requires hard work.

I work in Silicon Valley where some companies go from nothing to something quite rapidly. And the people who joined when it was nothing are often promoted very quickly into expanding roles as the company grows. And sometimes they are promoted faster than their ability to learn. One example I have seen over and over is when a talented engineer who developed the product's core code is promoted to a manager. While that person is brilliant at coding, they were never taught how to manage people. I am often brought into companies to help them transition into managers and team leaders. It doesn't happen overnight.

Perform is breaking the project into its core parts so you are ready to walk onto the big stage. For Mt. Everest, it is assumed you have the skill and technical aspects, as you gained them during Iterate, but now you must organize the team, prepare the equipment, manage the logistics, then work your way to Kathmandu and climb to the top of the mountain. For the social entrepreneur starting up in Guatemala, they will have to develop a business plan, select a site, pull together a team, and open their shop. During Iterate, they would have done many of these tasks but on a smaller scale and potentially under someone's guidance. The future CEO for the Guatemala nonprofit was working and learning from other nonprofit CEOs as they built their business plan, so soon he could do that for his. Or for my run around Lake Tahoe, Iterate got me to the starting line while Perform gets me to the finish line.

BEHAVIORS (PERFORM)

The Perform pillar is broken into these three behaviors:

1 **Focus on your goal:** I stay focused, despite distractions, and accomplish what I originally envisioned.

2 **Persevere through tough times:** When problems occur, I understand what I can control or influence and persevere through challenging situations.

3 **Aim higher:** In the end, I evaluate what worked and what could be improved, then think about what my next big achievement will be.

Chapter 13

FOCUS ON YOUR GOAL

> "Focus does not mean saying yes; it means saying no to the hundred other good ideas."
> **Steve Jobs**, founder, Apple Computer

IT IS NORMAL TO BE NERVOUS. Remember, you are doing something big—really big—and you may be going into unchartered territory. But isn't that what you signed up for? By now you should have done your homework and prepared, so proceed according to your plan.

NERVOUS IS NORMAL

In one of my interviews, successful psychologist and executive coach John Schinnerer, PhD, was helping his thirteen-year-old daughter. Her soccer team was playing in a competitive tournament, and the first round ended in a three-way tie for first place, which required a penalty kick shootout to decide the winners. While she was one of the best players, understandably she was scared and didn't want to fail, be embarrassed, or let her team down.

John pulled her aside, took off his sunglasses, looked her in the eyes and said, "I understand that you are nervous. That's normal. That's your body giving you energy to help you with this challenge. If it's too much energy, simply exhale longer than you inhale and imagine breathing out your extra energy. It doesn't matter to me if you make the shot or not. What matters to me is that you try. I will not let you back out of this because you are nervous. That is not how I want you to go through life. Fear is normal. Courage is feeling your fear and doing what you need to do in spite of that fear. YOU are brave. YOU are courageous. YOU can do this as you have prepared. Have fun with it. And breathe."

When it was her turn, she took a deep breath and placed the ball on the spot. The goalie got set. The referee blew the whistle. She ran three steps to the ball and struck it cleanly, and the ball hit the back of the net—Goooooooaaaalllll!!!

She had taken that shot in practice hundreds of times. She knew how to approach the ball, when to pull her leg back, where to connect her foot to the ball, and how to follow through with her kick. She had planned to be in this position, and now that she was, she just needed to have confidence in her plan and the hours of practice before this point. And that confidence comes from successfully completing the task many times before.

GIVE YOUR PLAN A CHANCE

While it is common to get to the starting line and see what others are doing, it is often a bad decision to make a change. Others around you may have a different plan, and you must have confidence in YOURS and stick with it. Don't panic just because you see someone else doing something different. Granted, you may have to shift course at some point, but give yourself a chance to succeed. If it doesn't initially work, gather data,

PILLAR V — PERFORM

get feedback, and more thoroughly assess your situation before making a fundamental shift. Be careful of pivoting too early. Remember what Shane Kenny said: "Most people fail right before they were to succeed because they just gave up."

When I stepped up to the starting line of my first fifty-miler, I had a plan to run for the first six miles and then go into a run-walk routine. I would run for nine minutes and then walk for one minute. I would continue with that strategy for the next forty-four miles. My friend, who was also running a fifty-miler

> "Most people fail right before they were to succeed because they just gave up."
>
> **Shane Kenny,** cofounder of InternetSafety.com, entrepreneur, and beach club owner

for the first time, hadn't thought too much about his plan but figured he would run as long as he could, then walk.

He was in much better shape than I physically, so at mile six, I said goodbye to him as he ran on, and I started to walk for one minute. It is actually hard to walk that early because you are feeling great, and you are watching everyone pass you by as they run when you could keep up with them. But I knew this was best FOR ME.

At mile thirteen he was about thirty seconds ahead of me. At mile twenty-six, he was about a minute ahead of me. And at mile thirty-two, I passed him as he was experiencing significant pain and barely walking. He almost quit at mile forty, but his crew encouraged him to keep going. Before the race, I predicted he would beat me by an hour. I came in two hours ahead of him. It wasn't because I was a better runner or in better shape. He was. But I did know what would work for me and had a more well-thought-out plan and stuck to it.

REMOVE THE NOISE AND STAY FOCUSED

We can often go further than we think, but we must stay focused on the goal. About five years into my career, I decided to start my MBA. It was a long-term goal and one I had set well before starting my undergraduate. But I wanted to make sure I got some "real-world" experience on my resume so the MBA had more meaning. I knew it would take more than the normal two years, as I was working full-time and only able to take one or two classes at night. Partway through, I took on a major project at work that was to last over a year and was causing me to stay in the office later and come in on the weekends. Between work and school, I had very little time for other activities and was starting to feel burnt out.

I started evaluating if I should take a break and resume classes when the project was over in a year. I had known many others who felt as I did and took a break but never returned to classes. I did not want that to happen. Fortunately, with summer approaching, I would get a short break. I kept focusing on the goal and knew that if I persevered for only one year, I would be done. If I took a break, the one year would go by, but I would have made no progress. Removing that noise in my head allowed me to refocus on my goal. Sometimes the noise isn't just in your head.

Tim Weyland, who is the CHRO for a midsize technology company and former professional soccer referee, knows about removing the noise. Literally. While refereeing professional soccer matches around the world, he often heard thousands of fans screaming. In some instances, they were rooting for the home team, sometimes they were harassing the other team, and most of the time they were yelling at him and the bad call they believed he just made. As Tim told me, "Basketball players can shut out the ten thousand people waving flags in front of them. I thought about this a lot while refereeing and how I had to focus on what is on the field."

Imagine being LeBron James getting ready to shoot a free throw in the final game and in the final minutes. Thousands of fans yelling obscenities, waving shirts, and jumping up and down only thirty feet in front of him are hoping he misses. His ability, as well as Tim's, is a skill that is learned. So imagine the noises you will face on your path to victory and ask yourself, *How can I turn the volume down so they don't get in the way of my concentration?*

FIND THE EXTRA GAS IN THE TANK

Jorge Angel is an Ironman athlete and record-holder for the fastest person to swim the true width of Lake Tahoe. He experienced this firsthand. During an Ironman competition, he had just completed the first loop of a two-loop run, indicating he had 13 miles left. He had already swum 2.4 miles, biked 110 miles, and run 13 miles, so he was understandably tired. Any event that makes you lap through the finish line and leave is difficult because mentally when you see the finish line you think, "It's time to stop." Your mind plays terrible tricks. When Jorge finished the first lap, he could hear the roar of the crowd cheering for those who were finishing, but he still had 13 miles to run. He would see his friends and family waiting for him but knew that he had to keep going for one more lap. While physically he had the energy, his mind was done. But he thought back to when he was seventeen years old.

As he recounted the story to me, he explained what got him through to the finish. He said,

> When I was seventeen, I was representing my country— Colombia—in the finals of one of the largest South American swimming competitions. The Peruvian in the lane next to me was pushing me to my limits. I kept up, but every hundred meters I thought, "When will this be over?" I was at my max and was not sure if I could sustain this pain for 1,500 meters. As my competitor came into the last flip turn, he thought he

was done and stopped. I took a slight lead before he realized his mistake, and then he caught me. And then he passed me. I was exhausted but dug deeper than ever before and touched the wall just before he did. I won and broke the state record that day, which was the highlight of my swimming career. As they put the gold medal around my neck, I heard my country's national anthem. When I find myself in difficult moments and find I cannot keep moving like that afternoon of the Ironman, I think back to when I was seventeen years old and wearing a gold medal around my neck listening to my national anthem. It helps me go a little further.

Coincidentally, Jorge was tested again when he beat the record for the fastest swim across the width of Lake Tahoe. As he approached the last few miles of the twelve-mile swim, his crew, which in a safety boat twenty feet away and following him the entire time, noticed that if he sped up slightly, he would break the record. Instead of telling him to speed up, they just slightly increased the speed of the boat. Not knowing the boat was going faster but having a harder time keeping up, he too sped up just a little until he maintained the pace of his boat. It was a gutsy move by the crew, but it worked, as he broke the record by six minutes. Had the boat captain not increased the speed, causing Jorge to go faster, that record may never have been broken. When tested, we can find the strength to go further. Jorge has proven that many times, as has the research.

> "When I find myself in difficult moments...I think back to when I was seventeen years old and wearing a gold medal around my neck listening to my national anthem. It helps me go a little further."
>
> **Jorge Angel,** Ironman athlete

Sport, exercise, and rehabilitation professor Florentina Hettinga, in her study referenced earlier, found cyclists competed 2 percent faster than their fastest known time when competition exists. We can go faster than we think. You have likely heard the stories of a man who lifts a car to save a trapped child. The adrenaline kicks in, and he is able to accomplish something he could never replicate. Somehow, we find *extra gas in the tank* or a *boost in performance*. We can go further than we think. Kevin Chou proved this in a different way.

When Kevin landed his dream job as a technology investment banker, he thought everything was going perfectly. Then he was laid off. He went on to a variety of roles, including playing poker to pay the rent, then working at a startup. He loved the startup and began to create his own business plan to put free games on the Internet. But he wasn't completely fulfilled. Kevin told me that he "knew I wouldn't have pushed myself if I didn't start my own company, and then I wouldn't be fulfilled." He went on to explain how he "knew how to be a VC but had no idea how to be a CEO, and this would put me into a really uncomfortable position." But pushing himself further was the best way to fulfillment. Apparently, this worked well for Kevin, as he went on to be the founder or cofounder of two other technology companies.

ACTIVITIES

QUESTIONS TO ASK YOURSELF

> How will you know you are on track?

> What "noise" or distractions are impacting your ability to move forward?

> Where are you most confident in your preparation? Least?

> What benefits will you receive when you arrive at the "finish line"?

EXERCISES

> Write down strategies to reduce the noise.

> Write down strategies to increase your confidence in areas where you feel less prepared.

Chapter 14

PERSEVERE THROUGH TOUGH TIMES

> "If the house burns down, you still have the foundation. That is your WHY."
> **Simon Sinek,** author

SHIT WILL HAPPEN. And many times, the fan will blow it all over the place and cause a terrible mess. It stinks. Your job is to think about what could go wrong, minimize the chances that it will, and then be prepared to deal with the mess when it occurs. If you assessed your obstacles in **Plan** and then managed those obstacles under **Iterate**, the chance of something going terribly wrong in **Perform** is significantly reduced. But something will go wrong. I guarantee it.

A person's ability to complete amazing things often is not about their willingness to keep going but their fortitude to not stop. Continuing is hard; stopping is easy. On a one-hundred-mile run through the Sierra mountain range and with only a marathon left to go, I was tired. It was the middle of the night; I was also cold, hungry, and irritable; and I had to pee. I came into the aid station, grabbed an energy bar, and went directly to the well-used, overly odiferous Port-a-Potty and sat down. I was in heaven, as I was off my feet, in a warm place, filling my belly, and emptying my bladder. I did not want to leave, but I knew that by sitting in my dark, warm, cozy oasis I was not moving any closer to the finish line. Expectations are drastically reduced seventy-five miles into a one-hundred-mile run when you find the inside of a Port-a-Potty the better option.

While most of us do everything possible to get in and out of those stinky boxes of bacteria as quickly as possible, I wanted to stay. Stopping would have solved a temporary problem of sore legs and a tired body, but I would have had a longer-term disappointment two days later when I saw DNF (Did Not Finish) next to my name. Stopping is easy. Finishing is hard. I got up, left my sanctuary, and continued down the trail.

A year later and only five days before the start of this run, I was faced with a more daunting challenge. My wife received some terrible news. In what we thought was a routine mammogram, the doctor saw something unusual. Hearing the word "cancer" is a shock the first time it goes into your ears. I am sure it is also a shock the second time as well.

After receiving the initial news that Monday morning, I said to my wife and biggest supporter, "Maybe we should cancel the Tahoe 200, and I'll try next year." Without a pause, she said, "We're going because there is nothing we can do about it between now and next week. You have trained too hard, and we have given so much to not do this." Two days later, and on our way to Tahoe, we stopped at the hospital for further testing. We were told the results would likely come after the race was over.

Remember when I said problems will occur? This was now my biggest challenge, one I wouldn't have dreamed of planning for, and I hadn't even started running. My wife wasn't giving me an excuse to quit, so I needed to persevere through this unexpected test. Remember all those excuses I talked about at the beginning of the book? I couldn't let one of them stop me.

SEE THE PIECES OF THE PUZZLE

Sometimes it is good to focus on the big things. And while that is one strategy, sometimes you must focus on the little things when all is not going smoothly. This happened to Phil Mumford, who spent most of his career as a middle-school teacher. But throughout his life, he has completed many long-distance bicycling adventures, including cycling across America multiple times and cycling throughout many European countries. He also completed Tour d'Afrique, a 7,500-mile ride from Cairo, Egypt, to Cape Town, South Africa (north to south on the African continent), at the age of sixty-three. While the beginning of these trips is often the hardest, he thought he bit off more than he could chew on the second day. For the first time in his life as he was riding along the Red Sea, he was thinking he made a terrible mistake and wondered, "How can I quit and get my money back?" Knowing that Cape Town was four months away, he looked at his insurance policy, which said he would need to have a broken leg to get a refund. "Broken leg, huh?" he thought.

That was not a good option, but he was having a difficult time wrapping his mind around how far the trip was as the headwinds blew against his face. He had to break the trip down into smaller segments. "I broke the trip into eight stages, which were still too daunting. So I broke it down even further from rest day to rest day (about five-day segments). That was still too long. Even day by day was too long. I finally settled into half-day segments and focused on getting to lunch. Then, I focused on getting to dinner. After 119 lunches and 119 dinners, I finally made it into Cape Town, South Africa."

All Across Africa cofounder Alicia Wallace also knows firsthand about challenges. As she and her cofounder were growing the business, they hit many roadblocks. Most of their workforce is based in Rwanda, a sub-Saharan African country of twelve million people. Their employees weave beautiful, handcrafted baskets that are then exported around the world to stores you have likely visited. When Ebola hit Africa, it also severely impacted Alicia's business, and they almost went under. I initially interviewed her before COVID, so now she has experienced two pandemics. Alicia, who is very methodical and driven to a plan, looked at this as a "big puzzle that I needed to put together." Instead of looking at the whole puzzle, she was able to focus on each piece and keep the business moving forward.

Matt Glerum had a similar situation on a particularly difficult paddle when he and his team capsized their outrigger canoe. When you flip your boat in big waves out in the middle of the ocean, it can freak someone out. Needing to solve that problem quickly, Matt got each person focusing on one piece of the puzzle. He assigned everyone a job. One person made sure everyone was safe. Another focused on getting the boat upright. Another person focused on emptying the boat. Once people can focus on their piece of the puzzle, the job replaces the unproductive fear and shifts to more productive activity.

Big problems are hard to solve, so break them down to smaller, more manageable, more easily solvable pieces.

I had a similar situation to Phil's on day one of my fifty-day, four-thousand-mile cycling trip across the US. While sitting in my tent the first evening after sixty miles of riding, I pulled out the US map to see how far I had gone. We used paper maps in those days, as Google Maps was seventeen years from being released. Sixty miles is not extremely far on a US map, about the width of my finger, which caused me to be discouraged as it appeared I hadn't gone very far toward my goal. I put the map away and said to myself that I would not pull it out until I had ridden one thousand miles and then only focused on regional or state maps. Sometimes it is good to look at the big picture, but then sometimes it can be so overwhelming that you need to zoom in much tighter.

GET THE STINK OUT OF THE BOAT

It is important to know what will turn you around and get you refocused. You knew when you signed up for the race, started that company, or set this goal it would be hard. Remember how Matt and a team of five colleagues entered the treacherous and challenging Yukon River Quest? It is in one of the most remote places in the world, and you must be prepared in case something goes wrong. Something will go wrong, and you will feel like shit. One moment you may be sweating, and the next moment a storm comes in, and the rain is pelting against your face, cooling your body more than it should. At the beginning your hands look beautiful while at the end they are covered in blisters, gauze, and blood. You knew that going in, so expect it to be hard and know what will pick you up when those times hit.

Two common phrases used by outrigger canoe paddlers when someone is emotionally drained and things aren't going well are to say, "Get your head in the boat" or "Get the stink out of the boat." They fundamentally mean the same thing, which is to focus on paddling. Matt explained: "For the River Quest, we made rules about what happens when there is 'stink in the boat,' meaning when problems were occurring, or someone was having a tough time. Each person gets three minutes of bitching and screaming. Someone will pay attention to the time and the rest of the team will help move the person to a better place."

Whatever is causing you to not focus on paddling needs to get out of your head. Matt relayed a story during one race at the beginning when several of the boats were jockeying for position and another boat hit his.

Tempers flared. His teammates were pissed. The steersman calmly said to everyone, "Get the stink out of the boat." He was mad, his teammates were mad, but that anger was not going to move them forward, and he wanted them to stop worrying about what already happened. He was letting his team know that the best thing we can do is let it go and move on.

When things go wrong, it is good to have already talked about what you can or will do. For Matt and his team, one thing was that short phrase. What is it for you? Is it listening to music, eating a bite of a chocolate bar, looking at a picture of a loved one? What will get your *stink out of the boat*? Sometimes you need a longer break, so take a weekend to remove yourself from the situation. Everyone has different needs, but recognize that going through hard times is normal, and it's OK to need a "pick-me-up."

I have always loved music, and some songs can help me move forward. I have two playlists for when I run. One is called "Run," which has a bunch of upbeat songs that I enjoy. I update these regularly. I then have a playlist called "Run Help," which are those songs I love and will lift me up. But if I overplay them, they will lose their impact. So I only pull them out during the darkest hour. During an especially difficult time in Tahoe, I turned my iPod to that rarely used playlist and let the tears flow as I thought of my wife and her possible cancer diagnosis. Two hours later, all was better. Not great but better.

Another highly successful strategy to get your head in the boat is to practice mindfulness.

Every morning my wife gets up and meditates for twenty minutes. During days when the kids are driving her crazier than normal, she finds this centers her and allows her to be calmer. I have tried this many times, and about two minutes into my meditation, my mind starts to wander onto something less peaceful—such as my next adventure, a cool project I am working on, or a project that needs to be done. It's not that I

PILLAR V — PERFORM

can't meditate; it's just that I haven't made it a big enough priority to regularly follow through in that aspect of my life.

When I tend to be a little less calm and lacking the patience that comes so naturally to her and not so much to me, she often suggests I take a breath and calm myself down. She is right. And when I stop, breathe, and slow my heart rate down, I feel better. I'm more relaxed, and I'm a better person. I hate it how she is always right. You'd think by now I'd realize how smart she is.

In discussion with Laurie Bodine, founder and CEO of START Leadership, she talked about how she uses "mindfulness to slow her brain down to reset her space and shift from a reactive to proactive state." In times of crisis, we tend to react to what is going on around us and let the crisis take control. So being mindful allows us to get a better handle on the situation and more effectively manage our emotions and our responses. She explained how "ten minutes of mindfulness at work offers significant benefits." This was also reinforced in a *Harvard Business Review* article, "Spending 10 Minutes a Day on Mindfulness Subtly Changes the Way You React to Everything." It states:

> Mindfulness practice decreases activity in the parts of the brain responsible for fight-or-flight and knee-jerk reactions while increasing activity in the part of the brain responsible for what's termed our executive functioning. This part of the brain, and the executive functioning skills it supports, is the control center for our thoughts, words, and actions. It's the center of logical thought and impulse control. Simply put, relying more on our executive functioning puts us firmly in the driver's seat of our minds, and by extension our lives.
>
> One second can be the difference between achieving desired results or not. One second is all it takes to become less reactive and more in tune with the moment. In that one

second lies the opportunity to improve the way you decide and direct, the way you engage and lead. That's an enormous advantage for leaders in fast-paced, high-pressure jobs.[36]

Some people don't meditate but pray. Some will quietly sit outside and listen to the birds. Some sit in a comfortable position and listen to relaxing music. Some repeat a mantra. What most of these "mindfulness" practices have in common is that you are in a peaceful place, you are sitting still, and you are focusing on something pleasant. The goal is to move your mind into a better space and slow your heart rate down. Figure out what works for you. I have had anxiety attacks in the past, and when I feel them coming on, these strategies work really well.

> "Ten minutes of mindfulness at work offers significant benefits."
>
> **Laurie Bodine,** founder and CEO of START Leadership

THERE'S A LIGHT AT THE END OF THE TUNNEL

The more you iterate and practice, the better you will do when problems occur. We need to be prepared for hard times. In most cases, it will get better. While it may get worse for a period, it will more than likely eventually improve. A friend found a lump on her breast and went in to have it biopsied. As she was sitting waiting for the test, the nurse came up, held her hand, and said, "I don't know if it is cancer or not, but let me tell you one thing. The next six to twelve months will suck, but after that, it will improve. You will have a long and productive life." She was setting her expectations. Knowing that there will be times when it is hard, you are miserable, and you are questioning whether you can move forward or get out of the jam. This is normal. And if you think about it beforehand, when the shit does hit the fan, you will at least have thought, "I knew this was going to happen, and I know I will get through it."

For those who have run a marathon, the wheels usually come off the bus between miles 20 and 22. That is often considered the "half-way" point of the 26.2-mile race. Most runners will tell you that if you get past those few miles, then the finish will be enjoyable. But at mile 20 when you start to feel like crap, and then at mile 21, you are questioning whether running a marathon was a good idea, and you begin to think about quitting. Surprisingly, at mile 23 you feel much better. This is normal. If you know this going into the run, you also know that you just must power through those few miles, and life will be much better in a short time. If you do not know about this phenomenon, then you may just quit. And if these don't work, keep in mind someone is likely facing bigger obstacles than you.

GRAB YOUR OWN PROBLEMS

I have traveled all over the world and been in some countries where kids do not have enough food. Where a cyclone recently came through, demolishing the town and everyone's homes. Where families are so poor, they mutilate their children so those kids can beg on the streets and get more money. Where girls are used as sex slaves. It is heart wrenching and difficult to see, but it is some people's reality. So when I am facing a difficult situation, I put my challenges in perspective compared to what others are facing. I then rarely feel bad for my situation.

At mile 156 of the 205-mile run around Lake Tahoe, when I was lying on the ground screaming as the medic was cleaning up one of the seven blisters on my feet—some the size of a quarter—and in great pain, wondering if I could continue, I then thought of my friend who found a lump on her breast, and the biopsy diagnosed it as breast cancer. My pain would more than likely be over in twenty-four to forty-eight hours when I reached the finish line. Hers would last a long time. I voluntarily put myself in this situation. She didn't. I could stop at any time. She couldn't. This conversation I had with myself helped me put things in perspective. Yes, my situation sucked, and I was in a lot of pain, but this helped me realize how fortunate I was that things weren't worse. I am not suggesting you deny your feelings whether emotional or physical, but I am suggesting to think through how what you are going through relates to what could be.

As my wife relays a story from a book she read, "If a group of us were sitting around the table and we all took our problems and threw them into the center of the table and then had to choose a problem to take back, chances are we would grab our own problems."

I thought a lot about this during our year in isolation because of COVID. My kids were having a hard time learning from home. We couldn't travel. We couldn't have friends over for dinner. We couldn't go to the movies. We couldn't…. It was far from ideal, but my kids could still "attend" school—virtually. I still had money in my bank account, food in the refrigerator, Netflix on the TV, my parents close by, and an amazing partner by my side. My problems paled in comparison to what so many others around the world, or even around the block, were going through. I was experiencing *First-World Problems.*

WORRY WON'T GET RESULTS

Henry Wadsworth Longfellow said, "The best thing one can do when it's raining is to let it rain." You can't control the rain, but you can control whether you get wet. Stay inside, wear a jacket, or put up your umbrella.

As the COVID cases started to decrease, vaccinations were approved, and life was looking better, I called Alicia Wallace and asked her how she was doing. The calm, levelheaded leader I talked to before COVID was still just as calm and levelheaded. When COVID hit, she thought back on what she learned from the Ebola crisis and kept telling herself, "We can't control everything. We survived Ebola, and we can survive this as long as we focus on what we can control." She was right. We tend to get frustrated by things we can't control and lose our ability to focus our attention on more important tasks.

I have always enjoyed watching the evening news. As a kid, it would generally come on once about dinner time. And then in the 1980s and 1990s, the twenty-four-hour cable news networks entered the picture. Initially, I thought this was great, as I could find out what was happening at any minute of the day. So when major stories are occurring, I find myself paying a little more attention to the TV.

During the coronavirus pandemic, for many months news networks only aired information about that one story. And about every half hour, they would repeat the same information. They would interview another doctor who would say the same thing as the previous doctor, and then on the bottom ticker or the sidebar would be the up-to-date death count or the number of people who had contracted the virus. After a commercial break, those numbers would go up. And since I was stuck at home, the news was on a lot. I found myself feeling anxious. Early on I changed my behavior and sheltered in place, washed my hands more often, used hand sanitizer after the rare instance when I did venture to the store. I was being much more cautious. But at a certain point, there was not much I could do differently. I realized that watching the news was 1) not informing me with anything new, 2) not changing my behavior, and 3) causing me to worry more. While I did not have control over what was happening in the world, I did have control over what I watched.

Dr. Michael Tompkins, PhD, UC Berkeley professor and codirector for the San Francisco Bay Area Center for Cognitive Therapy, refers to this as productive worry versus nonproductive worry. My nonproductive worry had escalated to an unhealthy level as watching the news was causing more harm than good. I grabbed the remote control and hit "Off."

I could not control how many people died or got sick. I could not control the massive spread of the virus. I could not control the constant repeating of the same message by the same doctor by the same news outlet. But I could control what I watched.

People bought up all the toilet paper because that is what they could control. While it may seem irrational, cognitively it makes sense. When I coach executives through major change initiatives, I explain that people have a difficult time adapting to change because they lack control. If we can take more control of the situation, we can then start to feel better.

Here are three questions I give to those executives to either ask themselves or ask the people they are guiding through something new:

> What could I GAIN through this situation? LOSE?
> Since I cannot control the situation fully, what can I influence?
> What next steps should I take?

Find out what aspects of the situation you can control or at least have some influence over. If you need to know something, find out who you can ask. It is not easy to mentally put aside all the things you cannot control, so take it in small bites as you plot your next steps.

As I left the starting line at nine that Friday morning and thought of my wife and her cancer diagnosis, I kissed her goodbye and tried to move those thoughts to the far reaches of my brain. Occasionally, they would move to the front and then be replaced by an aching muscle or a growing blister. Dealing with this run would be hard enough. Wondering if my wife had breast cancer only added to the difficulty, and I could never have predicted that would be an issue when I set this goal.

Twenty-one hours and seventy miles into this race, those thoughts came back with a vengeance and hit me hard. I had just run through the night and taken a caffeine pill to get me through the day when I felt the tears run down my cheeks. I turned to my playlist, "Run Help." Throughout the next 130 miles, I practiced mindfulness and focused on getting to the next aid station, when I would see my crew, instead of focusing on the finish line. I thought about all the people going through far more difficult times than I, which allowed me to turn a bad situation better. Not great, but better. Great would come four days later when we got the news everything was benign. I spent a lot of time worrying about something I did not need to worry about.

WHEN YOU FALL, GET UP

Throughout anything daunting, you will face adversity, you will be challenged, you will experience setbacks, and you may fall. When you fall, dust yourself off, look around to learn what you tripped on, and then move on. Two hundred miles into this epic 205-mile run and with just over five miles remaining, I went down and hit the ground hard. I was trying to maintain my top-ten position in the race and pushed myself as the eleventh-place runner was rapidly approaching. As I crested the last summit at almost 8,500 feet above sea level and started down the steep, treacherous trail to the finish line, my toe hit a rock, and down I went. As I hit the ground, the powderlike dirt poofed up around me and stuck to every part of my sweat-covered body. My wife, when she saw me at the finish line, said I looked like Pig-Pen from Charlie Brown. I slowly got up and noticed blood running down my arm. The eleventh-place runner, after checking if I was OK, passed me by. For a moment I was disappointed— disappointed that I missed out on top ten. The next mile was hard. But as

I continued down the hill, I began reflecting on this amazing accomplishment and realized that one fall should not define an entire race.

By falling, I was pushing myself. I remembered that time as a kid after a long day skiing in Colorado, and my dad said, "If you don't fall, you likely aren't pushing yourself hard enough." I was pushing myself.

> "If you don't fall, you likely aren't pushing yourself hard enough."
>
> **Roy Gillette,** fantastic dad

In those seventy-six hours, I ran 205 miles with only ninety minutes of sleep. In a marathon, you generally hit the wall once around mile 20. I hit several walls, but each time I climbed over them. Walls are a natural part of life, and some people are stopped by them. Others either go around or over them. That race was a microcosm of the emotional, cognitive, and perhaps spiritual toll of an EPIC Performance. I dug into my toolbox to find ways to cope. When one tool didn't get the job done, I sought out another. When it was over, I had another example of how I was capable of pursuing big things...and it got me thinking about what bigger things might be in store.

ACTIVITIES

QUESTIONS TO ASK YOURSELF

> How do you find your "Happy Place" when life is not so happy?
> How does this difficult time compare against your worst experience in life?
> What will allow you to get up and move forward?
> What aspects of the situation do you have control or influence over?
> How have others successfully made it through similar problems?

EXERCISES

> Identify two to three things you can implement when the going gets tough and you want to quit.
> Seek guidance from someone who has been through a similar difficult time.
> Try meditating daily over two weeks.

Chapter 15

AIM HIGHER

> "The difference between people who achieve their dreams and those who don't is simple. It's about action."
>
> **Sara Blakely,** CEO & founder, Spanx

As one accomplishment ends, it is time to think about what you want to accomplish next. Perform is not only about reaching the finish line and celebrating your accomplishment but starting to think about what's ahead. Or as climber and professional photographer Jimmy Chin says, "I've always been inspired by people who have pushed the upper limits of what is humanly possible. And when you look into it, they took an idea and took it up a notch and then took it up another notch."

CELEBRATE GOOD TIMES, C'MON

Who doesn't like a good celebration? Whether it is a big party with champagne, balloons, and all the fixings or a half gallon of ice cream, do something to acknowledge your success. Yes, my reward at the finish line after 205 miles was a shower, a nap, and a big bowl of mint chocolate chip ice cream…OK, three bowls.

Barbara Massa, chief people officer for security company FireEye, has long wanted to hold the top human resource job at a successful technology company. She spent many years taking on large projects that gave her the skills to do this and is a respected leader in the field. As Barbara told me, "I pictured myself ringing the bell (at Nasdaq). It wasn't because of the financial element, but it represented the pinnacle accomplishment of the business world." Several colleagues have expressed similar sentiments, and all whom I have known that have celebrated in this way worked hard to get there and deserved every moment. I remember how excited I was to be watching *CNBC Opening Bell with Jim Cramer* that morning and seeing Barbara. I can only imagine what she was feeling.

Most wait only until the very end to celebrate, but make sure to reward yourself and your team throughout the journey and at the success of each milestone.

Chris Henry, who led sales for a semiconductor manufacturer, knew this and would often hold beer and wine receptions in the office to celebrate significant quarterly revenue growth. He held many jobs, and at one point he was the coach for a top-flight international swimming team. On Friday mornings before practice, Chris would bring in a pillow with one red M&M to be awarded for the greatest practice effort. At the end of practice, the hardest-working athlete would be ceremoniously presented with the lone red M&M on top of the silk pillow. He was always amazed that people would swim to the brink of exhaustion for that

M&M. Sometimes the award does not have to be that big to generate incredible performance.

Did you feel the way you thought you would when you reached your goal? Was the emotional payoff as expected? I have told my kids many times to do things in life that make you cry when you accomplish them. Not tears of pain or sadness, although those may come too…but tears of joy. I remember running my first fifty-mile race with two friends. After the three of us successfully crossed the finish line and while we were lying down on the grass rubbing our sore muscles, I looked over at my buddies. They had tears in their eyes. Three grown men huddled around each other, all crying. That is a positive emotional payoff.

NEVER STOP LEARNING

At the end of your endeavor, it is time to sit down and evaluate your progress. In some cases, it will be after the champagne bottles are cleaned up and the party is over after you just accomplished something others said you couldn't do. And unfortunately, in other cases, it may be because the plan didn't work out as expected.

When things go as planned, or mostly to plan, look at your success and evaluate your performance. Even if you don't plan to replicate this goal again, those learnings could help you in other areas of your life. Or they could help the next person who comes to you and asks for guidance.

Failure does occur. Sometimes your business will go out of business. Sometimes you will not make it to the finish. Doctor, businessman, and hundred-mile runner Harris Goodman has seen things go wrong in all areas. Sometimes the diagnosis is wrong, the prescription does not do what it is intended to, or the patient hears something quite different than was intended. He calls these "medical misadventures." They are not intentional but something to understand and reduce the chance of happening next time. To not assign blame and assess in a nonjudgmental manner, he asks:

> What went wrong?
> What was the root cause?
> How can I avoid it in the future?

That ability to learn was so prevalent in all whom I talked to. After one of Chris Henry's sales reps missed out on an order, instead of showing disappointment, he would simply ask, "What did you learn?"

CIO Erik Molitor's number-one piece of advice for people looking to take big leaps is to "be introspective." Identify an area of personal development and seek out opportunities to learn and improve. He was not alone in that advice, as many others said something similar.

THE CYCLE CONTINUES: ENVISION AGAIN

Razmik Abnous had an amazing twenty-year journey with Howard Shao, his cofounder of the content management firm Documentum. After selling the company that he never dreamed would grow so big and so successful, he thought, "This is enough. I'm going to go travel a bit." And while he did travel "a bit," he started to fidget and wanted to explore what was next. It was a common trait I saw with several entrepreneurs who had significant financial exits and could safely retire. It is not about the money but the need to keep exploring and, for Razmik, tinker with technology.

Robert Owens, whom SEALFIT labeled "The Toughest and Fittest 66-Year-Old in the World," is still pushing the limits. While most people have slowed down, Robert seems to be ramping up. In the year he turned sixty-six, he ran across Greece, swam twenty-six miles in nine hours, and became the oldest finisher of the fifty-hour nonstop Navy SEAL Hell Week Challenge. Oh, and the year before, he finished seven marathons in seven days on seven continents. When I asked him what was next, he said, "I want to do the splits."

Now is your time. Go back to your dream notebook in whatever form you store those crazy ideas. Start dabbling with where you spend your time and determine how you will go big.

Years ago, I envisioned what this book would be. Now that I've finished it, I ask myself, "What's next?"

I am not suggesting we must keep setting records, getting faster, going farther, or starting up new companies. But consider what dream you have that will keep you living longer. My dad retired at the young age of fifty over thirty years ago (I say that is "young" now since I passed that milestone a few years ago). Expecting to have many years ahead of him, he dug deep into woodworking. As a retired contractor who built some amazingly beautiful homes, he had solid skills. But he continued to hone his craft and learn more and to this day can still be found in the woodshop crafting up some new project. He isn't running across a finish line of some epic race or starting up a nonprofit but realizing a passion of building some amazing pieces of art. Life should be about living your passions and accomplishing your dreams that make you happy, that stretch your own definition of "big" a little farther.

ACTIVITIES

QUESTIONS TO ASK YOURSELF

› What will you do to celebrate your success?

› Were your worst fears realized?

› What worked well?

› What would you do differently next time?

› What question do you wish you asked before starting this goal?

› What other possibilities exist in your life?

EXERCISES

› Write down what worked well and what could be improved for future use.

› Update your bucket list.

› Choose the next big goal you want to tackle.

Epilogue

TURNING BEARS INTO BAMBI

WE HAVE COME A LONG WAY on this journey, and I hope you have a better understanding, increased confidence, more tools, and most importantly, a stronger desire to reach higher and attain those lifelong aspirations.

Pursuing goals when you dream big is hard, but that emotional journey you experience along the way should pay off as you cross over whatever "finish line" you are running toward. Remember how you felt when you achieved something that was difficult...some might have even said crazy?

Elated? Relieved? Exhausted? Proud?

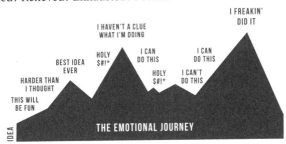

If that positive feeling you experienced at the end is greater than the negative feelings you faced on the road getting there, then wouldn't you agree that you made a wise decision to take on that challenge?

Are you ready for the next one…one that is even bigger, even crazier—no more excuses?

As you approach the end of one adventure (I freakin' did it!), start asking yourself, "What's next?" And if you feel butterflies in your belly and a bead of sweat drip down your brow, you are likely on the right track. You may not be able to be everything you always wanted to be, but now that you've gotten to the end of this book, you should be in position to apply what you've learned and reach higher peaks than ever before.

Remember, a growth mindset is a beautiful thing. Perhaps you saw those bears in your path that scared you at first but turned out to be friendly deer. Or heard yourself come up with some excuse for why you couldn't do something only to realize that maybe, just maybe, you can. And perhaps you stretched yourself further than you ever dreamed possible. Just like the muscles in your body, they may be strained and they may hurt, but more than likely, they will recover, then get stronger and allow you to jump even higher.

Don't forget that there are other people who are rooting for you to continue moving forward when you're tired. They're cheering for you to cross the finish line and be successful in whatever endeavor you have chosen.

All throughout your journey, someone—or many someones—gave you a nudge, shared a lesson from their experience, or picked you up when you fell. And just as they helped you reach your goal, consider whom you can now help reach theirs. While I find it highly rewarding to cross under the finisher's arch myself, in many cases I feel more rewarded to know I helped someone achieve their own dream.

Now is your time to pay it forward. Ask yourself, "Whom can I help?"

I wish you all the best in your next EPIC Performance and look forward to hearing about your triumphs—how you moved from "I can't" to "I did."

NOW, GO BE EPIC.

Overview of Interviews

THE PEOPLE I INTERVIEWED have achieved amazing results in many areas of their lives. What I found was they had a mindset to succeed in multiple areas. It should be no surprise then that as I talked to executives who were good at business, they also excelled in nonbusiness areas because they applied the same mindset, skills, and behaviors to other initiatives.

Over the course of one and a half years, I interviewed more than one hundred people who had reached the peak of their profession or were accomplished ultradistance endurance athletes or, in some cases, both. On the business side, in general, these were people who had reached the executive offices (e.g., CEO, CFO, COO, CHRO, CIO, or CMO) or were the president or founder of an organization. On the sport side, these were all amateur ultradistance athletes who had accomplished the equivalent of (or greater than) a full triathlon or 100-mile run. A full triathlon consists of a 2.4-mile swim, 26.2-mile run, and 112-mile bike ride. For instances in which a person did something other than a full triathlon or 100-mile run, I assessed if their accomplishment would require similar training and planning or more.

Eighty-six of those were structured interviews, all with the same questions, while the others were focused on specific topics. The gender split was 74 percent men and 26 percent women. The breakdown between business and sport was that 70 percent were business focused, 18 percent were sport focused, and 12 percent were both.

Lastly, I personally knew 64 percent of the interviewees prior to starting this project. As my last question was, "Is there anyone else you would recommend I talk to?", I was connected with other accomplished individuals.

The questions I asked were intended to generate responses where they needed to think through their goals and priorities and how they went about chasing their WHY. This was intended to assess an honest response about how they went after their goals personally or professionally. Below are the primary questions I asked:

> - I would like to understand when you have dreamed something big, then took it across the finish line.
> - There is a fine line between crazy and courageous. Where have you stepped on both sides of that line (or one side) and how did you differentiate between the two sides?
> - When did you find out you were on the wrong side of the line?
> - What is your view on risk?
> - What aspect of thinking, then doing, big do you feel you are strongest at? Weakest?
> - How do you adjust (overcome/develop) for your weaknesses?
> - What keeps you going when it becomes difficult?
> - What guidance would you have for someone trying to take big leaps?

These are most of the people I interviewed. Some names have been removed for those who have requested anonymity.

Razmik Abnous; David Alonso; Jorge Angel; Andrew Bartlow; Nikki Barua; Gerry Beemiller; Cath Bishop; Tim Blake; Laurie Bodine; Dan Boyle; Diann Boyle; George Brennan; Heather Brien; Barry Broome; Candra Canning; Kevin Chou; Keith Collins; Tracy Coté; Chris Crabtree; Julie Cullivan; Katey Dallosto; Alex Davis; Justin Davis; Rob Delange; Albert Dyrness; Dale Eldridge-Kaye; Jordan Epstein; Chris Fellows; Miguel Fernandez; Mike Freccero; Andy Frey; Mark Friedman; Audrey Gillette; Matt Glerum; Ken Gonzalez; Harris Goodman; Juliette Goodrich; Nadine Greiner; David Haglund; John Hamm; Brad Harris; Randy Haykin; Chris Henry; Jesse Hoag; Jack Jervoise; Bill Johnston; Aaron Kenny; Shane Kenny; Ilona Kinney; Paul Kinney; Fred Kitson; Thane Kreiner; Mark Lewis; James Lim; Kirsten Maplestone; Barbara Massa; Jeff Miller; Erik Molitor; Nancy Morehead; Phil Mumford; John Newton; Greg Novacek; Dave Osh; Jim Ott; Robert Owens; Jerry Pentin; Andy Perham; Lubor Ptacek; Bill Radulovich; Ralph Rajs; Ron Rel; Gordon Ritter; Bill Routt; Charles Scott; Howard Shao; Rob Shelton; Steve Sherman; John Schinnerer; Bruce Sinclair; Liz Steblay; Chris Stoner-Mertz; David Sweet; Laila Tarraf; Judy Tashbook; Bill Torchiana; Pat Torchiana; Luis Velasquez; Alicia Wallace; Tim Weyland; Bill Wheeler; Lindsey Williams; Liz Wiseman; Soon Yu.

Acknowledgments

As I write this section, I think of when an Academy Award winner walks onto the stage and is given forty-five seconds to thank everyone for their epic accomplishment. And then I think about how difficult that would be. Just forty-five seconds. That is essentially what I need to do in the following paragraphs by acknowledging all the people who helped get me to this point. Fortunately, I can recognize more people than the television audience—or the show's producer—would allow. I also realize that throughout this book I have encouraged you to push yourself to do what you felt was "impossible." I guess that is what I have to do, because mentioning everyone who helped me along the way truly does feel like an impossible task. But let me try.

The three most important people who supported me in realizing many of my crazy ideas, even when it wasn't in their best interests, were (and still are) my father, my mother, and my wife.

My parents gave me the confidence to push further and the runway to take off and fly. They encouraged me to go on adventures and experience life despite it making them nervous.

My father overcame more obstacles than I will ever know. He per세- vered through a childhood which few could have survived. While most people with his background died at an early age or found themselves in and out of jail, my dad went on to be a successful businessman, a sup- portive husband of over fifty-five years, and a loving father to me and my brother. In his eighties, he still hikes in the mountains, kayaks on reservoirs, travels the world, and spends time in the coffee shop with my mom or his two grandsons. My mother gave me my competitive edge and was a role model as I watched her play soccer well into her forties. She demonstrated her adventurous spirit by backpacking, kay- aking, bungee jumping, and performing all sorts of activities many of her generation never attempted. As I move through middle age, I still learn about what it means to be a better parent, a better spouse, and a better person because of them.

My wife, when I have a wild idea, is the first one to support me. She has shown me that saying "Yes" is much better than saying "No," even when "No" is the more prudent choice. She has washed my feet after 205 miles of running on dirt trails and hugged me when I smelled worse than one can imagine. She has been my travel partner around the world twice and the greatest life partner a person could ask for. I love her dearly.

I would also like to acknowledge my two boys, who have an exciting life ahead of them, and remind them to take full advantage of the time they have remaining on this planet. I know that when they hear of my next "great idea," they look at their mom and think, *Really, is that wise?* But I appreciate how they go along—in many cases they didn't have a choice—and seem to enjoy the journey. Someday they will thank us. I am hopeful they will continue to explore unfamiliar places and try new adventures. Along the way, they will fall, they will get hurt, and they will fall again. But I am hopeful they will get up, dust off their pants, learn from what just happened, and move forward. And then, that they eventually find their WHY.

Every Sunday, I meet up with a group of friends to either run, bike, hike, or walk up on a beautiful ridge a few miles from my house. As we get a little older, our pace is a little slower, but we still meet up. Many of these people trained with me for competitions. Some even did the unenviable job of pacing or crewing for me. The people I routinely see on a bike ride or run are: Jerry Pentin, Steve and Jan Sherman, Jim and Pam Ott, Stu Kron, Diann and Dan Boyle, Nancy Morehead, Kevin Greenlee, Jorge Angel, Liliana Perdomo, Bruce Sinclair, Jeff Hopkins, Marianne Paulson, and Ron Rel.

This book would be very short if not for the concepts, wisdom, and stories shared by all the people I interviewed. Some were colleagues, former bosses, mentors, friends, or friends of friends. Some were connected to me via my network, and had never met me before our interview. They all, however, shared personal stories and opened up about their challenges, their failures, and their successes. Most are mentioned in the Overview of Interviews section.

I have had many mentors along the way who helped mold me into the man I have become. The most impactful name was my boss, for whom I worked twice at Documentum, then at McAfee: Joe Gabbert. He taught me that I shouldn't wait for perfect.

Writing this was no easy task and took expertise from so many. While those mentioned above helped with the ideas for my manuscript and provided motivation when I wanted to stop, the following people made sure my words came together in this book. Thank you to the following folks at Amplify Publishing who helped me climb over the editorial and publishing mountain: Naren Aryal, Hobbs Allison, Myles Schrag, Brandon Coward, Shannon Sullivan, T.J. Carter, Gregg Baptista, Danny Moore, Kristin Perry, Sky Wilson, and Caitie Merico.

As I started this process years ago, I realized that writing and taking a book to market is similar to training for and running 200 miles. It was a great idea at the beginning—then it wasn't. Then it was. It was exhausting, challenging, exciting, daunting, and nerve-wracking. It was an emotional journey. There were days I wanted to stop and go on to other activities. But then I remembered why I was doing this and persevered to the finish line. I'm glad I did.

As the orchestra starts to play, indicating it is my turn to shut up and get off the stage, I will leave with one last note before we fade away. I've received a lot of support, as is evident by the number of people referenced earlier. Any errors in this book are not because of the names in this section but because of the name on the front cover. They are mine... not theirs. Thank you to all who have helped me get up the mountain... and safely back down to start the next adventure.

Fade to black...

Endnotes

1. "60 Minutes Presents: Going to Extremes," CBS News, February 26, 2012, https://www.cbsnews.com/video/60-minutes-presents-going-to-extremes/.

2. "Every Tour de France Winner Listed from Garin to Wiggins," *DataBlog* (blog), *Guardian*, July 23, 2012, https://www.theguardian.com/news/datablog/2012/jul/23/tour-de-france-winner-list-garin-wiggins#data.

3. Jonathan Alpert, *Be Fearless: Change Your Life in 28 Days* (New York: Center Street, 2012).

4. Alpert, *Be Fearless.*

5. "Accident Statistics," ICAO, https://www.icao.int/safety/iStars/Pages/Accident-Statistics.aspx.

6. "Protect Yourself and Loved Ones by Addressing Roadway Risks," National Safety Council (NSC), https://www.nsc.org/road-safety/safety-topics/fatality-estimates.

7. "Odds of Dying," National Safety Council (NSC), https://injuryfacts.nsc.org/all-injuries/preventable-death-overview/odds-of-dying/?.

8. "About Dyson: A New Idea," Dyson, https://www.lb.dyson.com/en-LB/community/aboutdyson.aspx.

9. "Explore Myths, Legends & Fun Facts of the Blue & Yellow Can," WD-40, https://www.wd40.com/myths-legends-fun-facts/.

10. Rachel Gillett, "How Walt Disney, Oprah Winfrey, and 19 Other Successful People Rebounded After Getting Fired," *Inc. Magazine*, October 7, 2015, https://www.inc.com/business-insider/21-successful-people-who-rebounded-after-getting-fired.html.

11. "Rejected Beatles Audition Tape Discovered," *Telegraph*, November 22, 2012, https://www.telegraph.co.uk/culture/music/the-beatles/9695499/Rejected-Beatles-audition-tape-discovered.html.

12. Bronnie Ware, *The Top Five Regrets of the Dying: A Life Transformed by the Dearly Departing.* (Hay House, 2019).

13. John Anderer, "Hindsight Is 20/20: 4 Out Of 10 Adults Regret Their Life Choices, Study Finds," July 22, 2019, https://www.studyfinds.org/hindsight-is-20-20-four-out-of-ten-adults-regret-their-life-choices/.

14. Jessica Stillman, "How Amazon's Jeff Bezos Made One of the Toughest Decisions of his Career," *Inc. Magazine*, June 13, 2016, https://www.inc.com/jessica-stillman/jeff-bezos-this-is-how-to-avoid-regret.html.

15. Ware, *Top Five Regrets.*

16. Rita Gunther McGrath, "The Pace of Technology Adoption is Speeding Up," *Harvard Business Review*, November 25, 2013, updated September 25, 2019, https://hbr.org/2013/11/the-pace-of-technology-adoption-is-speeding-up/.

17. Alpert, *Be Fearless.*

18. "What Is Exposure Therapy?," American Psychological Association, https://www.apa.org/ptsd-guideline/patients-and-families/exposure-therapy.

19. "What Is Exposure Therapy?"

20. Tom Ingram, "Managing Client/Server and Open Systems Projects: A 10-Year Study of 62 Mission-Critical Projects," *Project*

Management Journal 25, no. 2 (June 1994).

21. Ingram, "Managing Client/Server."

22. R. Discenza and J. B. Forman, "Seven Causes of Project Failure: How to Recognize Them and How to Initiate Project Recovery" (paper presented at PMI® Global Congress 2007—North America, Atlanta, GA, Newtown Square, PA: Project Management Institute, 2007).

23. Marky Stein, "Visualize Interview Success," Monster, https://www.monster.com/career-advice/article/interview-visualize-success.

24. *Kim Swims*, directed by Kate Webber (2017).

25. "S&P 500 Historical Annual Returns," Macrotrends, https://www.macrotrends.net/2526/sp-500-historical-annual-returns.

26. Alpert, *Be Fearless*.

27. Catherine Moore, "Learned Optimism: Is Martin Seligman's Glass Half Full?" Positive Psychology.com, November 2020, https://positivepsychology.com/learned-optimism/.

28. Moore, "Learned Optimism."

29. Alex Prewitt, "Tom Brady's Forgotten Rookie Year," *Sports Illustrated*, August 30, 2021, https://www.si.com/nfl/2021/08/30/tales-of-tom-brady-forgotten-rookie-year-2000-season-daily-cover#:~:text=Tom%20Brady%3A%20Inside%20his%20forgotten%20rookie%20season%20of%202000%20%2D%20Sports%20Illustrated.

30. Michael Lewis, "Obama's Way," *Vanity Fair*, September 11, 2012, https://www.vanityfair.com/news/2012/10/michael-lewis-profile-barack-obama.

31. "Collaborate," definition, *Merriam-Webster*.

32. "2020 Global Podcast Statistics, Demographics & Habits," PodcastHosting.org, May 23, 2020, https://podcasthosting.org/podcast-statistics/.

33. Marty Munson, "Make Your Competitiveness Work for You: Being

Competitive Can Be a Good and Bad Thing," *Swimmer Magazine,* September–October 2019.

34. Geoff Brumfiel, "Meet the Nuclear-Powered Self-Driving Drone NASA Is Sending to a Moon of Saturn," NPR, September 17, 2019, https://www.npr.org/2019/09/17/760649353/meet-the-nuclear-powered-self-driving-drone-nasa-is-sending-to-a-moon-of-saturn.

35. Michael Smith, "How Shackleton Recruited His Men," Shackleton, January 4, 2020, https://shackleton.com/blogs/articles/shackleton-recruitment.

36. Rasmus Hougaard, Jacqueline Carter, and Gitte Dybkjaer, "Spending 10 Minutes a Day on Mindfulness Subtly Changes the Way You React to Everything," *Harvard Business Review,* January 18, 2017, https://hbr.org/2017/01/spending-10-minutes-a-day-on-mindfulness-subtly-changes-the-way-you-react-to-everything.